He gives power to those who are tired and worn out; he offers strength to the weak. Even the young will become exhausted, and young men will give up. But those who wait on the Lord will find new strength. They will fly high on wings like eagles. They will run and not grow weary. They will walk and not faint.

Presented to

Chris Ulman

From

The Blackfords

Date

June 11, 2005

On the occasion of

High School Graduation

TouchPoints

for Graduates

TYNDALE

Copyright © 1996, 1999, 2001 by Tyndale House Publishers, Inc. All rights reserved.

Notes and special features copyright © 1996, 1999, 2001 by V. Gilbert Beers and Ronald A. Beers. All rights reserved.

Cover image copyright © by Artville. All rights reserved.

Questions, notes, and Scripture selection primarily by Jonathan Gray

Contributing writers: Rhonda O'Brien and Shawn A. Harrison

General Editors: V. Gilbert Beers and Ronald A. Beers

Designed by Julie Chen

Tyndale House Editor: Shawn A. Harrison

Portions of this book compiled from *The TouchPoint Bible,* copyright © 1996, and *TouchPoints for Students,* copyright © 1996, 1999 by Tyndale House Publishers, Inc.

Scripture quotations are taken from the *Holy Bible,* New Living Translation, copyright © 1996. Used by permission of Tyndale House Publishers, Inc., Wheaton, Illinois 60189. All rights reserved.

New Living Translation, the New Living Translation logo, and *TouchPoint* are registered trademarks of Tyndale House Publishers, Inc.

ISBN 0-8423-3612-5

Printed in the United States of America

09 08 07 06 05 04
5   4   3   2   1

Abilities

WHAT IS GOD'S PURPOSE IN GIVING US ABILITIES AND TALENTS?

2 Corinthians 1.21

It is God who gives us, along with you, the ability to stand firm for Christ.

Matthew 5.16

In the same way, let your good deeds shine out for all to see, so that everyone will praise your heavenly Father.

Philippians 3.9

I no longer count on my own goodness or my ability to obey God's law, but I trust Christ to save me. For God's way of making us right with himself depends on faith.

1 Corinthians 12.6-7

There are different ways God works in our lives, but it is the same God who does the work through all of us. A spiritual gift is given to each of us as a means of helping the entire church.

God gives us abilities so that we can bring honor to him. His gifts strengthen us to live for him, and they remind us that he is in control and is the giver of all things.

WHAT DOES GOD EXPECT US TO DO WITH THE GIFTS HE'S GIVEN US?

Luke 12:48

> *Much is required from those to whom much is given, and much more is required from those to whom much more is given.*

Romans 12:6

> *God has given each of us the ability to do certain things well. So if God has given you the ability to prophesy, speak out when you have faith that God is speaking through you.*

1 Corinthians 12:8

> *To one person the Spirit gives the ability to give wise advice; to another he gives the gift of special knowledge.*

Romans 12:8

> *If your gift is to encourage others, do it! If you have money, share it generously. If God has given you leadership ability, take the responsibility seriously. And if you have a gift for showing kindness to others, do it gladly.*

God expects us to use the gifts he's given us. He's given us abilities so that we can use them to help others know him.

WHY DOES IT SEEM THAT SOME PEOPLE HAVE SO MANY TALENTS AND ABILITIES, WHILE OTHERS DON'T HAVE AS MANY? CAN WE GROW OUR ABILITIES?

Matthew 25:15

> *He gave five bags of gold to one, two bags of gold to another, and one bag of gold to the last—dividing it in proportion to their abilities—and then left on his trip.*

Matthew 25:23

> The master said, "Well done, my good and faithful servant. You have been faithful in handling this small amount, so now I will give you many more responsibilities. Let's celebrate together!"

1 Timothy 3:10

> Before they are appointed as deacons, they should be given other responsibilities in the church as a test of their character and ability. If they do well, then they may serve as deacons.

God can entrust us with more as he chooses. When we choose to obey him and use our abilities in ways that please him, he may give us greater opportunities to make use of our talents.

PROMISE FROM GOD:

Philippians 4:13

> For I can do everything with the help of Christ who gives me the strength I need.

Abortion

WHEN DOES LIFE BEGIN?

Psalm 51:5

> I was born a sinner—yes, from the moment my mother conceived me.

The Bible makes it clear that life begins at conception, not merely at birth.

DID GOD REALLY WANT ME TO BE BORN? DOES HE HAVE A PLAN FOR ME?

Jeremiah 1:5

> *I knew you before I formed you in your mother's womb. Before you were born I set you apart and appointed you as my spokesman to the world.*

Psalm 139:13-16

> *You made all the delicate, inner parts of my body and knit me together in my mother's womb. Thank you for making me so wonderfully complex! Your workmanship is marvelous—and how well I know it. You watched me as I was being formed in utter seclusion, as I was woven together in the dark of the womb. You saw me before I was born. Every day of my life was recorded in your book. Every moment was laid out before a single day had passed.*

God not only knew all about you before you were born, but he wanted you to be born, and he has a plan for your life.

DON'T I HAVE THE FINAL SAY OVER WHAT HAPPENS TO MY BODY?

1 Corinthians 6:12-13

> *You may say, "I am allowed to do anything." But I reply, "Not everything is good for you." And even though "I am allowed to do anything," I must not become a slave to anything. . . . But our bodies were not made for sexual immorality. They were made for the Lord, and the Lord cares about our bodies.*

1 Corinthians 3:16-17

> *Don't you realize that all of you together are the temple of God and that the Spirit of God lives in you? God will bring ruin*

*upon anyone who ruins this temple. For God's temple is holy,
and you Christians are that temple.*

Our body is God's temple; his Spirit lives within us. Body,
mind, and heart must do what is honoring and pleasing to him.

IS ABORTION ABSOLUTELY WRONG?

Genesis 9:5

Murder is forbidden.

Proverbs 24:11-12

*Rescue those who are unjustly sentenced to death; don't stand
back and let them die. Don't try to avoid responsibility by
saying you didn't know about it. For God knows all hearts, and
he sees you. He keeps watch over your soul, and he knows you
knew! And he will judge all people according to what they have
done.*

Every child needs a champion, even the unborn child. If
abortion is taking the life of an unborn human being, then it is
murder, and it is absolutely wrong.

CAN GOD FORGIVE ME FOR HAVING AN ABORTION?

Isaiah 1:18

*No matter how deep the stain of your sins, I can remove it.
I can make you as clean as freshly fallen snow. Even if you are
stained as red as crimson, I can make you as white as wool.*

1 John 1:9

*If we confess our sins to him, he is faithful and just to forgive us
and to cleanse us from every wrong.*

Ephesians 3:18

> *May you have the power to understand, as all God's people should, how wide, how long, how high, and how deep his love really is.*

God can cleanse and heal us from any and all sin, no matter how big or terrible it might be.

PROMISE FROM GOD:

Jeremiah 1:5

> *I knew you before I formed you in your mother's womb.*

Absolutes

THERE SEEM TO BE SO MANY GRAY AREAS WHEN IT COMES TO RIGHT AND WRONG. HOW CAN I TELL WHAT IS REALLY RIGHT?

Exodus 20:1

> *Then God instructed the people.*

John 14:15

> *If you love me, obey my commandments.*

John 14:17

> *He is the Holy Spirit, who leads into all truth.*

Proverbs 21:2

> *People may think they are doing what is right, but the LORD examines the heart.*

Romans 8.5

> *Those who are dominated by the sinful nature think about sinful things, but those who are controlled by the Holy Spirit think about things that please the Spirit.*

Galatians 5.16

> *So I advise you to live according to your new life in the Holy Spirit. Then you won't be doing what your sinful nature craves.*

God has given us the Holy Spirit, who will help us live obediently. He will alert us when our old sinful nature is trying to take over. God has also given us his Word, the Bible, which clearly tells us absolute right and wrong.

SOME FRIENDS MAKE FUN OF ME FOR DOING RIGHT. HOW DO I DEAL WITH THAT?

1 Peter 3.14

> *Even if you suffer for doing what is right, God will reward you for it. So don't be afraid and don't worry.*

Genesis 18.19

> *Keep the way of the LORD and do what is right and just. Then I will do . . . all that I have promised.*

Romans 2.10

> *There will be glory and honor and peace from God for all who do good.*

Have you ever wondered why you feel good after doing something you know is right? That peace is God's promise to us for doing what is right.

PROMISE FROM GOD:

Timothy 3:16

All Scripture is inspired by God and is useful to teach us what is true and to make us realize what is wrong in our lives. It straightens us out and teaches us to do what is right.

Acceptance

HOW CAN I EARN GOD'S ACCEPTANCE?

Romans 3:27

Can we boast, then, that we have done anything to be accepted by God? No, because our acquittal is not based on our good deeds. It is based on our faith.

Colossians 2:6

And now, just as you accepted Christ Jesus as your Lord, you must continue to live in obedience to him.

We cannot earn God's acceptance. But his acceptance is available for free to you and everyone. All we do is believe that his Son, Jesus, died for our sins so that we could be free to enjoy eternal life with him. When we accept his forgiveness and ask him to be Lord of our life, he completely accepts us into his presence.

How do we learn to accept those who are different from us?

Matthew 9:11-12

> *"Why does your teacher eat with such scum?" they asked his disciples. . . . Jesus replied, "Healthy people don't need a doctor—sick people do."*

Every person is a unique creation of God, loved by God. If God loves everyone, shouldn't we?

What if a person has committed a terrible sin? Should we still accept him or her?

Romans 8:39

> *Nothing . . . will ever be able to separate us from the love of God that is revealed in Christ Jesus our Lord.*

Nothing we do can separate us from God's love. In the same way, we should always love others. This does not mean that we accept or condone their sinful actions, but we love and accept others as unique and special creations of God. It is only through love that we bring a sinful person back into fellowship with God and others. Even discipline must be carried out with loving motives.

What should we never accept?

2 Chronicles 34:4

> *He saw to it that the altars for the images of Baal and their incense altars were torn down.*

We must not accept or tolerate sin. Sin is our enemy, seeking to destroy us. If we allow any specific sin to dwell in our heart unattended, it will begin to spread like a malignant tumor, affecting all we think and do.

PROMISE FROM GOD:

Romans 15:7

> *Accept each other just as Christ has accepted you; then God will be glorified.*

Accomplishments

WHAT IS THE RIGHT PERSPECTIVE ON ACCOMPLISHMENTS?

Ecclesiastes 12:13

> *Here is my final conclusion: Fear God and obey his commands, for this is the duty of every person.*

Obeying God is life's greatest accomplishment.

IS ACCOMPLISHMENT JUST THE FRUIT OF HARD WORK, OR IS THERE SOMETHING ELSE TO IT?

Romans 1:17

> *This Good News tells us how God makes us right in his sight. This is accomplished from start to finish by faith. As the Scriptures say, "It is through faith that a righteous person has life."*

Getting ready for heaven, preparing for eternity in God's heavenly home, is not accomplished by any work we do but simply by faith, believing that Jesus Christ died for our sins so that we wouldn't have to. Salvation, this greatest of accomplishments, is not the work of our hands but the work of God in our heart.

WHAT IS A GOOD MODEL FOR ACCOMPLISHING THINGS?
Isaiah 25:1

> *O LORD, I will honor and praise your name, for you are my God. You do such wonderful things! You planned them long ago, and now you have accomplished them.*

God planned before he accomplished—a good model for us to follow.

HOW DO WE MAKE THE MOST OF OUR ACCOMPLISHMENTS?
Ecclesiastes 4:9

> *Two people can accomplish more than twice as much as one; they get a better return for their labor.*

It is impossible for one person to play a duet or a trio. It is hard to play football or soccer without teamwork. It is hard to have a happy marriage if only one mate works at it. Two people can actually do more than twice as much as one—as long as they are pulling in the same direction.

IS IT WRONG TO BE PROUD OF OUR ACCOMPLISHMENTS?
1 Corinthians 4:7

> *What makes you better than anyone else? What do you have that God hasn't given you? And if all you have is from God, why boast as though you have accomplished something on your own?*

There is a healthy satisfaction from accomplishment, which includes thanksgiving to God for what he has done through us. But it is arrogance to think we did the deed all by ourselves.

PROMISE FROM GOD:

Psalm 60:12

> *With God's help we will do mighty things.*

Accountability

HOW DO I BECOME MORE ACCOUNTABLE?

Psalm 119:9, 66

> *How can a young person stay pure? By obeying your word and following its rules. . . . Now teach me good judgment and knowledge.*

Psalm 1:1

> *Oh, the joys of those who do not follow the advice of the wicked.*

Proverbs 27:6

> *Wounds from a friend are better than many kisses from an enemy.*

To become more accountable, follow God's commands as outlined in his Word, the Bible. And choose wise friends with whom you can feel free and safe to give an account of yourself.

WHAT HAPPENS WHEN THERE IS NO ACCOUNTABILITY?
Judges 17:6
> *The people did whatever seemed right in their own eyes.*

1 Samuel 13:11-12
> *Saul replied, "I saw . . . you didn't arrive when you said you would. . . . I felt obliged to offer the burnt offering myself."*

Left unaccountable, we will always lean toward sin.

HOW CAN WE CHOOSE PEOPLE TO HOLD US ACCOUNTABLE?
1 Kings 12:8-10
> *Rehoboam rejected the advice of the elders and instead asked the opinion of the young men who had grown up with him. . . . The young men replied, "[Tell them] 'If you think he was hard on you, just wait and see what I'll be like!'"*

Our closest friends may not always be the best advisers, especially if their counsel is not consistent with God's Word.

HOW CAN I EFFECTIVELY HOLD SOMEONE ELSE ACCOUNTABLE?
Exodus 18:21-22
> *Find some capable, honest men who fear God and hate bribes. . . . They will help you carry the load, making the task easier for you.*

Titus 1:7-8
> *He must not be arrogant or quick-tempered. . . . He must live wisely and be fair. He must live a devout and disciplined life.*

If we are going to serve others by holding them accountable, we must be wise, honest, godly, and trustworthy.

DOES GOD REALLY HOLD US ACCOUNTABLE FOR ALL OUR ACTIONS?

Ecclesiastes 11:9

> *Young man, it's wonderful to be young! Enjoy every minute of it. Do everything you want to do; take it all in. But remember that you must give an account to God for everything you do.*

Enjoy life, but stay within God's guidelines. God will hold us accountable for everything we do, and who wants to explain ungodliness to a holy God on the Day of judgment?

PROMISE FROM GOD:

1 John 2:3

> *How can we be sure that we belong to him? By obeying his commandments.*

Advice

WHY DO I NEED ADVICE FROM OTHERS? I KNOW WHAT I'M DOING.

Proverbs 12:15

> *Fools think they need no advice, but the wise listen to others.*

Wisdom involves recognizing our own inadequacies. Foolishness is thinking we have none.

How valuable is wise advice?
Proverbs 25:11
> *Timely advice is as lovely as golden apples in a silver basket.*

Timely advice is not merely helpful; it is beautiful. It is not merely beautiful; it is essential.

Where do I look for good advice?
Genesis 6:9
> *Noah was a righteous man. . . . He consistently followed God's will and enjoyed a close relationship with him.*

Titus 1:15
> *Everything is pure to those whose hearts are pure.*

Seek advice from those who are faithful, godly, honest, and trustworthy. They can be counted on to give you counsel that comes from God's Word.

How do I evaluate the advice of others?
Matthew 7:16
> *You can detect them by the way they act, just as you can identify a tree by its fruit.*

2 John 1:9
> *If you wander beyond the teaching of Christ, you will not have fellowship with God.*

One way to evaluate advice is to evaluate the adviser. Do the adviser's words and life produce good fruit or bad? When evaluating advice, check it against the truth of God's Word. If it contradicts the Bible, then it is bad advice.

How do I give good advice to others?
Philippians 4:8

> *Fix your thoughts on what is true and honorable and right.*
> *Think about things that are pure and lovely and admirable.*
> *Think about things that are excellent and worthy of praise.*

When giving advice to others, have pure motives, point to God's Word, and don't use advice as an excuse to lecture. Pray about what you want to say, and have the other's best interests in mind. Words are like medicine; they should be measured with care. An overdose may do more harm than good.

What happens when I follow good advice?
Psalm 1:1

> *Oh, the joys of those who do not follow the advice of the wicked,*
> *or stand around with sinners, or join in with scoffers.*

Following evil advice leads to sorrow and disaster, robbing us of joy and satisfaction. Godly advice leads to good results, enriching our joy.

Promise from God:
Psalm 32:8

> *I will guide you along the best pathway for your life. I will*
> *advise you and watch over you.*

Affirmation

How does God affirm us?

Genesis 1:27

> God created people in his own image; God patterned them after himself; male and female he created them.

1 Peter 2:5

> God is building you, as living stones, into his spiritual temple. What's more, you are God's holy priests, who offer the spiritual sacrifices that please him because of Jesus Christ.

1 Corinthians 15:3

> I passed on to you what was most important and what had also been passed on to me—that Christ died for our sins, just as the Scriptures said.

God created us, so he understands our need for affirmation. He values us so much that he was willing to send his Son to die for us because he wants us to live with him forever.

How do we affirm others?

1 Thessalonians 5:11

> Encourage each other and build each other up, just as you are already doing.

Romans 14:19

> Let us aim for harmony in the church and try to build each other up.

Hebrews 7:7

> *Without question, the person who has the power to bless is always greater than the person who is blessed.*

Galatians 5:13-14

> *You have been called to live in freedom—not freedom to satisfy your sinful nature, but freedom to serve one another in love. For the whole law can be summed up in this one command: "Love your neighbor as yourself."*

We affirm one another through encouragement, praise, and building each other up. This gives us a great sense of worth.

PROMISE FROM GOD:

Psalm 67:1

> *May God be merciful and bless us. May his face shine with favor upon us.*

AIDS

WHY IS THERE AIDS?

Genesis 3:19

> *All your life you will sweat to produce food, until your dying day. Then you will return to the ground from which you came. For you were made from dust, and to the dust you will return.*

When Adam and Eve disobeyed God's command, all of life changed. Sin entered the world, and as a result there is sickness, pain, and death. AIDS, like any disease, is a result of living in a fallen world.

WHAT SHOULD OUR RESPONSE BE TO PEOPLE WITH AIDS?
2 Corinthians 2:6-7

> *He was punished enough when most of you were united in your judgment against him. Now it is time to forgive him and comfort him. Otherwise he may become so discouraged that he won't be able to recover.*

Matthew 22:39

> *Love your neighbor as yourself.*

Romans 12:9

> *Don't just pretend that you love others. Really love them. Hate what is wrong. Stand on the side of the good.*

Regardless of how someone acquired AIDS, we must treat that person with the same love that Christ would show.

WHAT IS OUR RESPONSIBILITY TOWARDS OTHERS WITH AIDS?
Mark 6:34

> *A vast crowd was there as he stepped from the boat, and he had compassion on them because they were like sheep without a shepherd.*

2 Corinthians 1:4

> *He comforts us in all our troubles so that we can comfort others. When others are troubled, we will be able to give them the same comfort God has given us.*

God calls us to love, serve, and have compassion for all people.

PROMISE FROM GOD:

Romans 8:39

> *Nothing in all creation will ever be able to separate us from the love of God.*

Anger

WHY DO WE USUALLY GET ANGRY?

Numbers 22:29

> *"Because you have made me look like a fool!" Balaam shouted.*

We get angry when our pride is hurt.

Genesis 4:4-5

> *The LORD accepted Abel and his offering, but he did not accept Cain and his offering. This made Cain very angry and dejected.*

We get angry when someone else gets more praise or attention than we do.

2 Chronicles 26:18-19

> *"Get out of the sanctuary, for you have sinned." . . . Uzziah was furious and refused to set down the incense burner he was holding.*

Esther 3:2-5

> *Mordecai refused to bow down or show [Haman] respect. . . .*
> *[Haman] was filled with rage.*

We get angry when we don't get our way.

1 Samuel 18:8

> *This made Saul very angry. "What's this?" he said. "They credit*
> *David with ten thousands and me with only thousands."*

We get angry when we become jealous of what others have or
what they have done.

1 Kings 22:18-27

> *"Didn't I tell you?" the king of Israel said. . . . "He never*
> *prophesies anything but bad news for me. . . . Put this man*
> *in prison, and feed him nothing but bread and water."*

We get angry when we are confronted about our sinful actions
and are exposed.

WHEN IS IT OK TO BE ANGRY?

John 2:15-16

> *[Jesus] drove out the sheep and oxen, scattered the money*
> *changers' coins . . . and . . . told them, "Get these things out*
> *of here. Don't turn my Father's house into a marketplace!"*

Numbers 25:11

> *Phinehas . . . has turned my anger away from the Israelites*
> *by displaying passionate zeal among them on my behalf.*

Anger at sin is not only appropriate but necessary.

WHEN WE ARE ANGRY, WHAT SHOULD WE AVOID?

James 3:5

The tongue is a small thing, but what enormous damage it can do.

Avoid speaking your mind when you are angry. You are bound to say something you will regret.

1 Samuel 19:9-10

As David played his harp for the king, Saul hurled his spear at David in an attempt to kill him.

Avoid acting on impulse in the heat of anger. You are bound to do something you will regret.

WE ALL GET ANGRY AT TIMES, SO WHAT SHOULD WE DO ABOUT IT?

Ephesians 4:26-27

Don't sin by letting anger gain control over you. Don't let the sun go down while you are still angry, for anger gives a mighty foothold to the Devil.

Anger is like a wild skunk in the house. We shouldn't feed it to encourage it to stay. And we should try to get rid of it as soon as possible.

PROMISE FROM GOD:

Psalm 103:8

The LORD is merciful and gracious; he is slow to get angry and full of unfailing love.

Apathy

WHAT HAPPENS IF APATHY IS ALLOWED TO GROW IN OUR LIFE?

Jeremiah 12:4

> *How long must this land weep? Even the grass in the fields has withered. The wild animals and birds have disappeared because of the evil in the land.*

Without God, our life becomes empty and withered. We become focused on ourselves, and all our relationships suffer. The way to keep apathy from taking root in your life is to set aside time daily for study of God's Word and prayer.

PROMISE FROM GOD:

2 Timothy 1:7

> *God has not given us a spirit of fear and timidity, but of power, love, and self-discipline.*

Appearance

HOW IMPORTANT TO GOD IS MY OUTWARD APPEARANCE?

Proverbs 31:30

> *Charm is deceptive, and beauty does not last; but a woman who fears the LORD will be greatly praised.*

1 Samuel 16:7

> *People judge by outward appearance, but the LORD looks at a person's thoughts and intentions.*

James 1:23

> *If you just listen and don't obey, it is like looking at your face in a mirror but doing nothing to improve your appearance.*

Outward beauty reveals what we look like. Inner beauty reveals who we are. Walking with God causes us to reflect his beauty from within.

CAN I TRUST PEOPLE BASED ON THEIR APPEARANCE?

Isaiah 53:3

> *He was despised and rejected—a man of sorrows, acquainted with bitterest grief. We turned our backs on him and looked the other way when he went by. He was despised, and we did not care.*

Matthew 23:28

> *You try to look like upright people outwardly, but inside your hearts are filled with hypocrisy and lawlessness.*

Appearances can often be misleading. Jesus came to earth as a man and was rejected and murdered by his chosen people. Be careful not to judge people based on how they look.

HOW IMPORTANT IS IT TO MAINTAIN A GOOD APPEARANCE?

Colossians 3:17

> *Whatever you do or say, let it be as a representative of the Lord Jesus, all the while giving thanks through him to God the Father.*

Matthew 7:20

> *Yes, the way to identify a tree or a person is by the kind of fruit that is produced.*

As representatives of Christ, how we present ourselves is important, but even more important is the condition of our heart and the actions that result.

PROMISE FROM GOD:

1 Samuel 16:7

> *The LORD looks at a person's thoughts and intentions.*

Astrology

IS ASTROLOGY WRONG?

Exodus 20:3

Do not worship any other gods besides me.

2 Kings 21:6

Manasseh even sacrificed his own son in the fire. He practiced sorcery and divination, and he consulted with mediums and psychics. He did much that was evil in the LORD's sight, arousing his anger.

Occult practices, including astrology, involve worshiping other gods, which is why these practices arouse God's anger.

CAN ASTROLOGY GIVE US DIRECTION?

Genesis 1:16-17

God made two great lights, the sun and the moon, to shine down upon the earth. . . . He also made the stars. God set these lights in the heavens to light the earth.

Don't seek advice from the stars, but from God, the Creator of the stars. Only he can give you direction for your life, because he created you, too.

WHAT DO I DO WHEN I'VE FALLEN AWAY FROM GOD?

Amos 5:4

> This is what the LORD says to the family of Israel: "Come back to me and live!"

Romans 3:23-24

> All have sinned; all fall short of God's glorious standard. Yet now God in his gracious kindness declares us not guilty. He has done this through Christ Jesus, who has freed us by taking away our sins.

Because of our sinful nature, there are times when we all fall away from God. Yet once we've identified and confessed our sin, God is faithful to forgive us. There is no sin so great that we cannot come back to God.

HOW CAN I AVOID BACKSLIDING?

Ezekiel 37:23

> They will stop polluting themselves with their detestable idols and other sins, for I will save them from their sinful backsliding. I will cleanse them. Then they will truly be my people, and I will be their God.

1 Peter 1:14

> Obey God because you are his children. Don't slip back into your old ways of doing evil; you didn't know any better then.

Matthew 26:41

> *Keep alert and pray. Otherwise temptation will overpower you.*
> *For though the spirit is willing enough, the body is weak!*

1 Corinthians 10:13

> *Remember that the temptations that come into your life are no*
> *different from what others experience. And God is faithful. He*
> *will keep the temptation from becoming so strong that you can't*
> *stand up against it. When you are tempted, he will show you a*
> *way out so that you will not give in to it.*

Obedience to God's Word, prayer, and being alert to temptation help us stay away from backsliding.

WHAT IS THE EFFECT ON OTHERS WHEN I BACKSLIDE?

Matthew 18:7

> *How terrible it will be for anyone who causes others to sin.*
> *Temptation to do wrong is inevitable, but how terrible it will*
> *be for the person who does the tempting.*

When we sin, it almost always affects someone other than ourselves. This is why we must call upon God to help us overcome the temptation to sin.

PROMISE FROM GOD:

Psalm 32:5

> *Finally, I confessed all my sins to you. . . . And you forgave me!*

Beauty

WHAT DOES GOD CONSIDER BEAUTIFUL?
1 Peter 3:4

> *You should be known for the beauty that comes from within, the unfading beauty of a gentle and quiet spirit, which is so precious to God.*

The more we reflect God, the more we radiate his beauty. What could be more beautiful than God's reflection?

HOW CAN MY WORDS BE BEAUTIFUL?
Proverbs 15:26

> *The LORD despises the thoughts of the wicked, but he delights in pure words.*

Proverbs 25:11

> *Timely advice is as lovely as golden apples in a silver basket.*

Beautiful words come from godly thoughts and character.

HOW CAN MY WORSHIP BE BEAUTIFUL?
Psalm 33:1

> *Let the godly sing with joy to the LORD, for it is fitting to praise him.*

Beautiful worship is the fruit of a beautiful relationship with God.

PROMISE FROM GOD:
Proverbs 19:22

> *Loyalty makes a person attractive.*

Behavior

WHAT DOES GOD EXPECT IN MY BEHAVIOR?
1 Timothy 4:12

> *Don't let anyone think less of you because you are young. Be an example to all believers in what you teach, in the way you live, in your love, your faith, and your purity.*

God wants each of us to be an example of Christ to others.

Romans 12:2

> *Don't copy the behavior and customs of this world, but let God transform you into a new person by changing the way you think.*

God expects to transform our behavior.

Romans 13:13

> *We should be decent and true in everything we do, so that everyone can approve of our behavior. Don't participate in wild parties and getting drunk, or in adultery and immoral living, or in fighting and jealousy.*

God expects us to live by a higher standard, which will meet with others' approval and bring glory to God.

How does my behavior affect others?

1 Samuel 20:34

> Jonathan left the table . . . and refused to eat all that day, for he was crushed by his father's shameful behavior toward David.

The selfishness of poor behavior often hurts the people we love the most.

Why is godly behavior so important?

Matthew 5:16

> Let your good deeds shine out for all to see, so that everyone will praise your heavenly Father.

Ephesians 4:32

> Be kind to each other, tenderhearted, forgiving one another, just as God through Christ has forgiven you.

Titus 2:12

> We are instructed to turn from godless living and sinful pleasures. We should live in this evil world with self-control, right conduct, and devotion to God.

When people see godly behavior in us, they will want to know what makes us different. We then have a wonderful opportunity to tell them.

Promise from God:

Luke 11:28

> Even more blessed are all who hear the word of God and put it into practice.

Bible

HOW CAN A BOOK WRITTEN SO LONG AGO BE RELEVANT FOR ME TODAY?

Hebrews 4:12

> *The word of God is full of living power. It is sharper than the sharpest knife, cutting deep into our innermost thoughts and desires. It exposes us for what we really are.*

2 Timothy 3:16-17

> *All Scripture is inspired by God and is useful to teach us what is true and to make us realize what is wrong in our lives. It straightens us out and teaches us to do what is right. It is God's way of preparing us in every way, fully equipped for every good thing God wants us to do.*

Isaiah 40:8

> *The grass withers, and the flowers fade, but the word of our God stands forever.*

Even though it was written long ago, the Bible is God's Word to us today, and it is relevant for our every need.

WHY IS IT IMPORTANT TO MEMORIZE PORTIONS OF SCRIPTURE FROM THE BIBLE?

Deuteronomy 30:14

> *The message is very close at hand; it is on your lips and in your heart so that you can obey it.*

Psalm 37:31

> *They fill their hearts with God's law, so they will never slip from his path.*

Psalm 119:11

> *I have hidden your word in my heart, that I might not sin against you.*

What you fill your heart and mind with is what you become. Memorizing Scripture helps you call God's life-changing words to mind at any time.

How can the Bible give me guidance?

Psalm 73:23-24

> *Yet I still belong to you; you are holding my right hand. You will keep on guiding me with your counsel, leading me to a glorious destiny.*

Psalm 119:105

> *Your word is a lamp for my feet and a light for my path.*

Proverbs 6:23

> *For these commands and this teaching are a lamp to light the way ahead of you. The correction of discipline is the way to life.*

James 1:5

> *If you need wisdom—if you want to know what God wants you to do—ask him, and he will gladly tell you. He will not resent your asking.*

The Word of God is from the mind and heart of God—and who can deny that the all-wise, all-powerful, ever-present God is the best guide of all?

How can the Bible give me comfort?

Psalm 119:49-50, 52, 54

> Remember your promise to me, for it is my only hope. Your promise revives me; it comforts me in all my troubles. . . . I meditate on your age-old laws; O LORD, they comfort me. . . . Your principles have been the music of my life throughout the years of my pilgrimage.

Proverbs 30:5

> Every word of God proves true. He defends all who come to him for protection.

Romans 15:4

> Such things were written in the Scriptures long ago to teach us. They give us hope and encouragement as we wait patiently for God's promises.

The Bible is filled with God's promises, which give us comfort and encouragement in this life, as well as the confident assurance that we will one day live forever in peace and security with him.

Promise from God:

Psalm 119:89

> Forever, O LORD, your word stands firm in heaven.

Blame

Is blaming others sin?

Genesis 3:12-13

> "Yes," Adam admitted, "but it was the woman you gave me
> who brought me the fruit, and I ate it." Then the LORD God
> asked the woman, "How could you do such a thing?" "The
> serpent tricked me," she replied. "That's why I ate it."

We often want to blame others for our sin. But God knows our
heart and is not fooled by our attempts to take the spotlight off
ourselves.

What can I do to live a blameless life?

1 Corinthians 1:8

> He will keep you strong right up to the end, and he will keep
> you free from all blame on the great day when our Lord Jesus
> Christ returns.

1 Thessalonians 3:13

> Christ will make your hearts strong, blameless, and holy when you
> stand before God our Father on that day when our Lord Jesus comes
> with all those who belong to him.

Colossians 1:22

> Now he has brought you back as his friends. He has done this
> through his death on the cross in his own human body. As a

*result, he has brought you into the very presence of God, and
you are holy and blameless as you stand before him without a
single fault.*

There is no way that we alone could ever live a blameless life.
It is only through Christ's dying on the cross that we are found
blameless.

SINCE IT IS IMPOSSIBLE FOR ME TO LIVE BLAMELESSLY, AM I FREED OF RESPONSIBILITY?

Philippians 2:15

*You are to live clean, innocent lives as children of God in a
dark world full of crooked and perverse people. Let your lives
shine brightly before them.*

Our responsibility is to live by Christ's example. We are to keep
our heart and mind pure. Imperfection is no excuse for perversion!

Boredom

HOW DO WE GET BORED?

Hebrews 6:11-12

*Our great desire is that you will keep right on loving others as
long as life lasts, in order to make certain that what you hope
for will come true. Then you will not become spiritually dull
and indifferent. Instead, you will follow the example of those*

who are going to inherit God's promises because of their faith and patience.

We get bored when we lose hope. It is hope that enables us to press on even when things are difficult.

WHAT ARE SIGNS OF BOREDOM?

Galatians 6:9

Don't get tired of doing what is good. Don't get discouraged and give up, for we will reap a harvest of blessing at the appropriate time.

Proverbs 26:14

As a door turns back and forth on its hinges, so the lazy person turns over in bed.

Ecclesiastes 2:23

Their days of labor are filled with pain and grief; even at night they cannot rest. It is all utterly meaningless.

Getting tired of what is good, a sense of meaninglessness, laziness—these are all signs of boredom.

WHAT ELIMINATES BOREDOM?

Romans 5:11

Now we can rejoice in our wonderful new relationship with God—all because of what our Lord Jesus Christ has done for us in making us friends of God.

Romans 8:28

We know that God causes everything to work together for the good of those who love God and are called according to his purpose for them.

Nehemiah 8:10
> *The joy of the LORD is your strength!*

Ephesians 5:1-2
> *Follow God's example in everything you do. . . . Live a life filled with love for others, following the example of Christ.*

God has a plan for each of us. Boredom disappears when our relationship with God grows to where we recognize his purpose for us. If we really try to follow Christ's example every day, we will never become bored!

PROMISE FROM GOD:
Philippians 2:4
> *Don't think only about your own affairs, but be interested in others, too, and what they are doing.*

Challenges

IN A WORLD THAT SEEMS OPPOSED TO GOD, HOW DO I HANDLE THE CHALLENGE OF KEEPING MY FAITH STRONG?
Psalm 40:12
> *Troubles surround me—too many to count! They pile up so high I can't see my way out. They are more numerous than the hairs on my head. I have lost all my courage.*

1 Chronicles 28:20

> *Be strong and courageous, and do the work. Don't be afraid or discouraged by the size of the task, for the LORD God, my God, is with you. He will not fail you or forsake you.*

Hebrews 6:18

> *God has given us both his promise and his oath. These two things are unchangeable because it is impossible for God to lie. Therefore, we who have fled to him for refuge can take new courage, for we can hold on to his promise with confidence.*

The strength to handle adversity comes from God alone. Therefore we must stay close to him through Bible study and prayer, never doubting his promises.

WHAT CAN I DO WHEN SOMEONE CHALLENGES ME?

Proverbs 15:31-32

> *If you listen to constructive criticism, you will be at home among the wise. If you reject criticism, you only harm yourself; but if you listen to correction, you grow in understanding.*

Galatians 2:11

> *When Peter came to Antioch, I had to oppose him publicly, speaking strongly against what he was doing, for it was very wrong.*

When someone challenges sin in our life, we must humbly look inside ourselves to determine whether the criticism is valid. We should be grateful to those who challenge us to live a godly life, and learn to discern when someone's challenge is not founded in truth.

WHAT IF SOMEONE DARES OR CHALLENGES ME TO DO WRONG?
Joshua 1:7

> *Be strong and very courageous. Obey all the laws Moses gave you. Do not turn away from them, and you will be successful in everything you do.*

2 Corinthians 13:8

> *Our responsibility is never to oppose the truth, but to stand for the truth at all times.*

Sin is often very attractive and very fun. If it wasn't, we wouldn't want to sin. One of our greatest challenges is to do right in the face of temptation, especially when it comes from friends.

HOW DOES GOD CHALLENGE US?
Mark 10:21

> *Jesus felt genuine love for this man as he looked at him. "You lack only one thing," he told him. "Go and sell all you have and give the money to the poor, and you will have treasure in heaven. Then come, follow me."*

God challenges us to examine our heart and make sure he has first place in our life.

PROMISE FROM GOD:
Psalm 37:5

> *Commit everything you do to the LORD. Trust him, and he will help you.*

I WANT TO HAVE GOOD CHARACTER, BUT SOME OF MY FRIENDS LAUGH AT ME FOR MY "CLEAN LIVING."
1 Corinthians 15:33

> *Don't be fooled by those who say such things, for "bad company corrupts good character."*

If our friends' influence keeps us from having good character, the answer is to get different friends who share godly values.

CAN'T I WORK ON MY CHARACTER WHEN I GET OLDER?
1 Timothy 4:12

> *Don't let anyone think less of you because you are young. Be an example to all believers in what you teach, in the way you live, in your love, your faith, and your purity.*

Godly character is simply a reflection of who we are. If you aren't interested in developing godly character now, you won't be interested in it later.

WHAT ATTRIBUTES ARE FOUND IN GODLY CHARACTER?
Ezekiel 18:5-9

> *Suppose a certain man is just and does what is lawful and right, and he has not feasted in the mountains before Israel's idols or worshiped them. And suppose he does not commit*

41

> adultery. . . . Suppose he is a merciful creditor . . . and does not
> rob the poor but instead gives food to the hungry and provides
> clothes for people in need. And suppose he grants loans without
> interest, stays away from injustice, is honest and fair when
> judging others, and faithfully obeys my laws and regulations.
> Anyone who does these things is just and will surely live, says the
> Sovereign LORD.

Godly character involves treating others with justice.

Galatians 5:22-23
> When the Holy Spirit controls our lives, he will produce this
> kind of fruit in us: love, joy, peace, patience, kindness, goodness,
> faithfulness, gentleness, and self-control.

Godly character includes all of the fruit of the Spirit.

HOW CAN I DEVELOP MY CHARACTER?

Deuteronomy 8:2
> Remember how the LORD your God led you through the
> wilderness for forty years, humbling you and testing you to prove
> your character, and to find out whether or not you would really
> obey his commands.

James 1:4
> So let [your endurance] grow, for when your endurance is fully
> developed, you will be strong in character and ready for
> anything.

We are not born with godly character; it is developed. We develop
our character by facing daily challenges and choosing wisely.

PROMISE FROM GOD:

Galatians 5:22-23

> When the Holy Spirit controls our lives, he will produce this kind of fruit in us: love, joy, peace, patience, kindness, goodness, faithfulness, gentleness, and self-control.

Cheating

WHAT DOES GOD THINK OF CHEATING?

Proverbs 11:1

> The LORD hates cheating, but he delights in honesty.

Cheating is the opposite of honesty because the motives behind it are always to deceive someone else. How can anyone trust a cheater?

CAN WE CHEAT OURSELVES?

Luke 16:10

> Unless you are faithful in small matters, you won't be faithful in large ones. If you cheat even a little, you won't be honest with greater responsibilities.

When we cheat, we are actually cheating ourselves out of what God has planned for us.

HOW DO WE CHEAT GOD?

Malachi 3:8

> *Should people cheat God? Yet you have cheated me! But you ask, "What do you mean? When did we ever cheat you?" You have cheated me of the tithes and offerings due to me.*

We cheat God when we don't give him what he rightfully deserves.

Choices

HOW DO I KNOW IF I AM MAKING GOOD OR BAD CHOICES?

Genesis 13:10-13

> *Lot took a long look at the fertile plains of the Jordan Valley in the direction of Zoar. The whole area was well watered everywhere. . . . Lot chose that land for himself. . . . Lot moved his tents to a place near Sodom, among the cities of the plain. The people of this area were unusually wicked and sinned greatly against the LORD.*

2 Peter 2:7-8

> *Lot . . . was a righteous man who was distressed by the wickedness he saw and heard day after day.*

Genesis 19:15, 30

> *The angels . . . said to Lot, " . . . Get out of here right now, or you will be caught in the destruction of the city." . . . Afterward Lot . . . went to live in a cave in the mountains.*

Genesis 25:33-34

> *Esau swore an oath, thereby selling all his rights as the firstborn to his younger brother. Then Jacob gave Esau some bread and lentil stew. Esau ate and drank and went on about his business, indifferent to the fact that he had given up his birthright.*

If our choices are being guided primarily by selfish ambition or a desire for physical fulfillment, it is very likely that we, like Lot and Esau, are making bad decisions.

1 Kings 12:8

> *Rehoboam rejected the advice of the elders and instead asked the opinion of the young men who had grown up with him and who were now his advisers.*

Proverbs 12:15

> *Fools think they need no advice, but the wise listen to others.*

If we reject the advice of proven wise counselors, like Rehoboam did, we are probably making a very foolish decision. But if we listen to advice and weigh it carefully, we are more likely to make good choices.

Proverbs 1:7

> *Fear of the LORD is the beginning of knowledge. Only fools despise wisdom and discipline.*

If our decisions are being guided by reverence for God, then we are on our way to making good choices.

Matthew 16:26

> *How do you benefit if you gain the whole world but lose your*
> *own soul in the process? Is anything worth more than your soul?*

If our choices are guided by a desire to gain the world, then we are probably going to make some very bad decisions.

John 5:19

> *Jesus replied, "I assure you, the Son can do nothing by himself.*
> *He does only what he sees the Father doing."*

If we, like Jesus, keep continually in mind what God would have us do, then we are more likely to make good choices that honor him.

Galatians 5:22-23

> *When the Holy Spirit controls our lives, he will produce this*
> *kind of fruit in us: love, joy, peace, patience, kindness, goodness,*
> *faithfulness, gentleness, and self-control. Here there is no conflict*
> *with the law.*

Good choices are always in keeping with the fruit of the Holy Spirit, while bad choices often involve rejecting his influence in our heart.

PROMISE FROM GOD:

Psalm 23:3

> *He guides me along right paths, bringing honor to his name.*

Church

WHY SHOULD I BE INVOLVED IN CHURCH?

Psalm 27.4

> *The one thing I ask of the LORD—the thing I seek most—is to live in the house of the LORD all the days of my life, delighting in the LORD's perfections and meditating in his Temple.*

Psalm 84.4

> *How happy are those who can live in your house, always singing your praises.*

Even though God lives in the heart of every believer, he commands us to gather with other believers. When we do that, we meet with God in a special way.

Ephesians 2.19-22

> *Now you Gentiles are no longer strangers and foreigners. You are citizens along with all of God's holy people. You are members of God's family. We are his house, built on the foundation of the apostles and the prophets. And the cornerstone is Christ Jesus himself. We who believe are carefully joined together, becoming a holy temple for the Lord. Through him you Gentiles are also joined together as part of this dwelling where God lives by his Spirit.*

All believers together form God's family, God's house, God's temple, and we are joined together. But only by meeting together can we experience this reality.

Hebrews 10:25

Let us not neglect our meeting together, as some people do, but encourage and warn each other, especially now that the day of his coming back again is drawing near.

When we meet together, we can build each other up and help each other. But we can't experience this kind of fellowship if we don't meet with others!

HOW IS THE CHURCH SUPPOSED TO FUNCTION TOGETHER?

Romans 12:4-6

Just as our bodies have many parts and each part has a special function, so it is with Christ's body. We are all parts of his one body, and each of us has different work to do. And since we are all one body in Christ, we belong to each other, and each of us needs all the others. God has given each of us the ability to do certain things well.

Ephesians 4:16

Under his direction, the whole body is fitted together perfectly. As each part does its own special work, it helps the other parts grow, so that the whole body is healthy and growing and full of love.

God intends the different members of the body to find their place and to function in their particular area of ministry so that the body can be spiritually healthy.

Ephesians 4:3-6

> *Always keep yourselves united in the Holy Spirit, and bind yourselves together with peace. We are all one body, we have the same Spirit, and we have all been called to the same glorious future. There is only one Lord, one faith, one baptism, and there is only one God and Father, who is over us all and in us all and living through us all.*

God desires unity and peace in the church because this accurately portrays the truth about God and our faith.

PROMISE FROM GOD:

Matthew 16:18

> *Upon this rock I will build my church, and all the powers of hell will not conquer it.*

Compassion

HOW DOES GOD SHOW HIS COMPASSION TO ME?

Psalm 103:8

> *The LORD is merciful and gracious; he is slow to get angry and full of unfailing love.*

Psalm 103:13

> *The LORD is like a father to his children, tender and compassionate to those who fear him.*

God shows his compassion to us by giving us blessings we don't deserve and by not giving us what we do deserve. Instead, he forgives us and restores us to what we were intended to be.

How can I show compassion to others?

2 Corinthians 8:9

> *You know how full of love and kindness our Lord Jesus Christ was. Though he was very rich, yet for your sakes he became poor, so that by his poverty he could make you rich.*

Christ in his love for us gave up his most high position to come to earth and die for us. Our response should be to throw out our pride and show compassion to those around us, even when doing so takes us out of our comfort zone.

Promise from God:

Psalm 72:12

> *He will rescue the poor when they cry to him; he will help the oppressed, who have no one to defend them.*

Competition

Is competition good or bad?

1 Corinthians 9:24

> *Remember that in a race everyone runs, but only one person gets the prize. You also must run in such a way that you will win.*

1 Corinthians 15:10

> *Whatever I am now, it is all because God poured out his special favor on me—and not without results. For I have worked harder than all the other apostles, yet it was not I but God who was working through me by his grace.*

Competition can drive us to improve ourselves or sharpen our skills. Paul certainly was competitive, and God used this in his life to reach people and establish churches throughout the world.

WHEN DOES COMPETITION BECOME A BAD THING?

2 Timothy 2:5

> *Follow the Lord's rules for doing his work, just as an athlete either follows the rules or is disqualified and wins no prize.*

Genesis 4:4-8

> *The LORD accepted Abel and his offering, but he did not accept Cain and his offering. This made Cain very angry and deject-ed. . . . Later Cain suggested to his brother, Abel, "Let's go out into the fields." And while they were there, Cain attacked and killed his brother.*

Competitiveness can lead to jealousy, anger, and bitterness, causing us to sin.

Luke 18:11

> *The proud Pharisee stood by himself and prayed this prayer: "I thank you, God, that I am not a sinner like everyone else, especially like that tax collector over there! For I never cheat, I don't sin, I don't commit adultery."*

Competition can lead us to compare ourselves with others. This is pride, and pride always leads us toward trouble.

ARE THERE AREAS WHERE COMPETITION IS NOT APPROPRIATE?
Matthew 18:1-4
> *About that time the disciples came to Jesus and asked, "Which of us is greatest in the Kingdom of Heaven?". . . Then [Jesus] said, ". . . Anyone who becomes as humble as this little child is the greatest in the Kingdom of Heaven."*

God looks upon us as having equal worth. Competition becomes inappropriate anytime it causes us to think we are more important than others.

PEOPLE SAY I CAN BE TOO COMPETITIVE AT TIMES. HOW CAN I LEARN TO LIGHTEN UP?
Matthew 6:19-20
> *Don't store up treasures here on earth. . . . Store your treasures in heaven.*

We are warned not to spend our life competing for the wrong things or for the wrong reasons.

Colossians 3:23
> *Work hard and cheerfully at whatever you do, as though you were working for the Lord rather than for people.*

We should work hard to do our best, not to beat others. Our best honors the God who created us.

PROMISE FROM GOD:

1 Corinthians 15.57

> *How we thank God, who gives us victory over sin and death through Jesus Christ our Lord!*

Complacency

WHAT CAUSES US TO GROW COMPLACENT?

Hosea 13.5-6

> *I took care of you in the wilderness, in that dry and thirsty land. But when you had eaten and were satisfied, then you became proud and forgot me.*

When we are in need, we usually take God more seriously. But when we are well fed, comfortable, and prosperous, it is easy to become complacent about God. Wise is the person who remembers God daily in times of both need and prosperity.

IS IT A SIN TO BE COMPLACENT?

James 4.17

> *Remember, it is sin to know what you ought to do and then not do it.*

God takes righteousness seriously. So should God's people. To know what is right and then be complacent about it or unwilling to do it is sin.

Revelation 3:15-16

> *I know all the things you do, that you are neither hot nor cold. I wish you were one or the other! But since you are like lukewarm water, I will spit you out of my mouth!*

Complacency leads to indifference, which leads to idleness. To stand for nothing is to stand against God. That's why complacency is so dangerous.

How can complacency lead us to sin?

1 Kings 11:1-3

> *King Solomon loved many foreign women. . . . The LORD had clearly instructed his people not to intermarry with those nations. . . . Yet Solomon insisted on loving them anyway. . . . And sure enough, they led his heart away from the LORD.*

Solomon's complacency toward God and God's commands led him into sin and its devastating consequences.

Promise from God:

Proverbs 1:32

> *Complacency will destroy them.*

Complaining

HOW SHOULD I REACT WHEN OTHERS COMPLAIN ABOUT ME?

Proverbs 15:31-32

> If you listen to constructive criticism, you will be at home among the wise. If you reject criticism, you only harm yourself; but if you listen to correction, you grow in understanding.

Proverbs 25:12

> Valid criticism is as treasured by the one who heeds it as jewelry made from finest gold.

Proverbs 29:1

> Whoever stubbornly refuses to accept criticism will suddenly be broken beyond repair.

We should always listen to criticism and seek to learn and grow from it.

WHAT SHOULD I DO INSTEAD OF COMPLAINING?

Philippians 2:14-15

> In everything you do, stay away from complaining and arguing, so that no one can speak a word of blame against you. You are to live clean, innocent lives as children of God in a dark world full of crooked and perverse people. Let your lives shine brightly before them.

Instead of complaining about others, be a role model to them. Role modeling at its best lifts others up, while complaining puts them down.

Lamentations 3:39-40

Then why should we, mere humans, complain when we are punished for our sins? Instead, let us test and examine our ways. Let us turn again in repentance to the LORD.

Instead of complaining about the sins of others, we ought to repent of our own sins.

Luke 6:37

Stop judging others, and you will not be judged. Stop criticizing others, or it will all come back on you. If you forgive others, you will be forgiven.

Instead of complaining about the weaknesses of others, we ought to forgive them as we would like to be forgiven.

WHAT IS IT ABOUT COMPLAINING THAT IS SO WRONG?

Numbers 11:1

The people soon began to complain to the LORD about their hardships; and when the LORD heard them, his anger blazed against them. Fire from the LORD raged among them and destroyed the outskirts of the camp.

Numbers 14:27-30

How long will this wicked nation complain about me? I have heard everything the Israelites have been saying. Now tell them this: "As surely as I live, I will do to you the very things I heard you say. I, the LORD, have spoken! You will all die here in this wilderness! Because you complained against me, none of you who are twenty years old or older and were counted in the census will enter the land I swore to give you."

1 Corinthians 10:10

> *Don't grumble as some of them did, for that is why God sent his angel of death to destroy them.*

God considers complaining a sin because it demonstrates an attitude of ungratefulness.

Deuteronomy 6:16

> *Do not test the LORD your God as you did when you complained at Massah.*

Complaining is often a form of testing God and his patience.

Job 10:1

> *I am disgusted with my life. Let me complain freely. I will speak in the bitterness of my soul.*

Complaining reveals an attitude of bitterness.

Psalm 106:25

> *Instead, they grumbled in their tents and refused to obey the LORD.*

Complaining can lead to further disobedience.

PROMISE FROM GOD:

Ephesians 4:29

> *Let everything you say be good and helpful, so that your words will be an encouragement to those who hear them.*

Compromise

WHEN IS COMPROMISE INAPPROPRIATE?

Romans 6:12

> *Do not let sin control the way you live; do not give in to its lustful desires.*

When compromise involves sin of any kind, it is inappropriate.

1 Samuel 15:24

> *Then Saul finally admitted, "Yes, I have sinned. I have disobeyed your instructions and the LORD's command, for I was afraid of the people and did what they demanded."*

Exodus 23:2

> *Do not join a crowd that intends to do evil.*

3 John 1:11

> *Dear friend, don't let this bad example influence you. Follow only what is good.*

Compromise is inappropriate when it is motivated by people pleasing or following the bad example of others.

WHAT IS A DANGER OF INAPPROPRIATE COMPROMISE?

Proverbs 25:26

> *If the godly compromise with the wicked, it is like polluting a fountain or muddying a spring.*

Exodus 34:12

> *Be very careful never to make treaties with the people in the land where you are going. If you do, you soon will be following their evil ways.*

Compromising with evil causes us to sin.

WHEN IS COMPROMISE APPROPRIATE, AND HOW DO WE EFFECTIVELY COMPROMISE?

Romans 14:15

> *If another Christian is distressed by what you eat, you are not acting in love if you eat it. Don't let your eating ruin someone for whom Christ died.*

A Christian must be willing to avoid those things that offend others in order to maintain unity in the body of Christ. This may require compromising personal preferences, but never Christian convictions.

Romans 15:1

> *We may know that these things make no difference, but we cannot just go ahead and do them to please ourselves. We must be considerate of the doubts and fears of those who think these things are wrong.*

Sometimes we should compromise so that we don't offend others or cause them to stumble in their faith.

Philippians 2:2

> *Make me truly happy by agreeing wholeheartedly with each other, loving one another, and working together with one heart and purpose.*

Sometimes we should compromise for the sake of unity in the church.

HOW DO I RESPOND APPROPRIATELY WHEN I AM TEMPTED TO COMPROMISE ABOUT WALKING IN GOD'S WAYS?

1 Corinthians 10:13

Remember that the temptations that come into your life are no different from what others experience. And God is faithful. He will keep the temptation from becoming so strong that you can't stand up against it. When you are tempted, he will show you a way out so that you will not give in to it.

1 Corinthians 16:13

Be on guard. Stand true to what you believe. Be courageous. Be strong.

Ephesians 6:11

Put on all of God's armor so that you will be able to stand firm against all strategies and tricks of the Devil.

It is never appropriate to compromise your Christian convictions.

PROMISE FROM GOD:

1 Corinthians 10:13

God is faithful. He will keep the temptation from becoming so strong that you can't stand up against it. When you are tempted, he will show you a way out so that you will not give in to it.

Conflict

HOW DO I KEEP CONFLICT WITH OTHERS TO A MINIMUM?

Proverbs 26:17

> *Yanking a dog's ears is as foolish as interfering in someone else's argument.*

It is sometimes tempting to become involved in an argument in progress in order to "solve it," but doing so often only heats up the issue.

Romans 12:18

> *Do your part to live in peace with everyone, as much as possible.*

As Christ's ambassadors we need to work actively to be at peace with others.

Ephesians 4:3

> *Always keep yourselves united in the Holy Spirit, and bind yourselves together with peace.*

Spiritual unity and fellowship with God through the Holy Spirit will often help us to bring unity and peace to our relationships.

WHAT IS THE RIGHT WAY TO HANDLE CONFLICT OR DISAGREEMENT?

Genesis 13:8-9

> *Then Abram talked it over with Lot. "This arguing between our herdsmen has got to stop," he said. "After all, we are close relatives! I'll tell you what we'll do. Take your choice of any section of the land you want, and we will separate. If you want that area over there, then I'll stay here. If you want to stay in this area, then I'll move on to another place."*

1 Corinthians 6:7

> *To have such lawsuits at all is a real defeat for you. Why not just accept the injustice and leave it at that? Why not let yourselves be cheated?*

Like Abram, we might have to give up what we want in order to resolve a conflict over personal interests.

John 17:21

> *My prayer for all of them is that they will be one, just as you and I are one, Father—that just as you are in me and I am in you, so they will be in us, and the world will believe you sent me.*

We should pray for peace and unity with other people.

Acts 15:37-39

> *Barnabas . . . wanted to take along John Mark. But Paul disagreed strongly, since John Mark had deserted them in Pamphylia. . . . Their disagreement over this was so sharp that they separated.*

Sometimes differences of opinion are so strong that no resolution seems possible and a parting of ways is necessary.

2 Timothy 2:24-25

The Lord's servants must not quarrel but must be kind to everyone. They must be able to teach effectively and be patient with difficult people. They should gently teach those who oppose the truth.

When people disagree with what we are saying, instead of becoming angry and defensive, we should maintain a gracious and gentle attitude.

PROMISE FROM GOD:

Psalm 55:18

He rescues me and keeps me safe from the battle waged against me, even though many still oppose me.

Conformity

WHY DOES GOD CALL US TO BE DIFFERENT?

2 Corinthians 5:17

What this means is that those who become Christians become new persons. They are not the same anymore, for the old life is gone. A new life has begun!

Christians are to act like Christ, who calls us to be loving, kind, and merciful.

1 Corinthians 8:9
> *You must be careful with this freedom of yours. Do not cause a brother or sister with a weaker conscience to stumble.*

Many people say, "I'm going to do what I want. I don't care what people say." But Christians can't have that attitude. They have a special responsibility to act as representatives of Christ. We should be concerned about what others say if our actions are not consistent with our faith. This could cause new believers to doubt what their faith is all about.

CAN WE CONFORM TO GOD AND STILL HANG ON TO OLD HABITS?

Luke 18:21-23
> *The man replied, "I've obeyed all these commandments since I was a child." "There is still one thing you lack," Jesus said. "Sell all you have and give the money to the poor, and you will have treasure in heaven. Then come, follow me." But when the man heard this, he became sad because he was very rich.*

In this parable God shows that it is very difficult for us to let go of the things of this world. Conforming to his standard is hard work and requires much from us, but it brings eternal rewards.

PROMISE FROM GOD:

2 Corinthians 5:17

> *What this means is that those who become Christians become new persons. They are not the same anymore, for the old life is gone. A new life has begun!*

Conscience

WHAT EXACTLY IS OUR CONSCIENCE, AND WHERE DOES IT COME FROM?

Romans 1:19-20

> *The truth about God is known to them instinctively. God has put this knowledge in their hearts. From the time the world was created, people have seen the earth and sky and all that God made. They can clearly see his invisible qualities—his eternal power and divine nature. So they have no excuse whatsoever for not knowing God.*

When God created humans, he created them in his image. This makes us unique compared with the rest of God's creation. Conscience is the God-given knowledge deep inside us that guides us between right and wrong. It is the part of us that helps us understand whether we are in line with God's will.

IF GOD CREATED EVERYONE WITH A CONSCIENCE, WHY HAVE SOME PEOPLE DONE SUCH HORRIBLE THINGS?

1 Timothy 1:19

> *Cling tightly to your faith in Christ, and always keep your conscience clear. For some people have deliberately violated their consciences; as a result, their faith has been shipwrecked.*

If we consistently go against what our conscience tells us, we can dull our conscience, making it hard and insensitive to sin.

CAN YOU LOSE YOUR CONSCIENCE?

Proverbs 28:17

> *A murderer's tormented conscience will drive him into the grave. Don't protect him!*

You can't lose your conscience, but you can become so dulled to its urgings that you don't or can't hear it. Even those who have done horrible deeds still have a conscience. But over time they have learned to tune it out. This is so dangerous because without your conscience you feel free to do whatever you want.

HOW CAN I DEVELOP MY CONSCIENCE?

Hosea 12:6

> *So now, come back to your God! Act on the principles of love and justice, and always live in confident dependence on your God.*

Even those who have rejected God can come back to him. When you commit yourself to God and live by the commands in his word, he will restore your conscience.

PROMISE FROM GOD:
Psalm 119:105
> *Your word is a lamp for my feet and a light for my path.*

Consequences

DOES SIN *ALWAYS* HAVE NEGATIVE CONSEQUENCES?
Isaiah 30:12-13
> *This is the reply of the Holy One of Israel: "Because you despise what I tell you and trust instead in oppression and lies, calamity will come upon you suddenly. It will be like a bulging wall that bursts and falls. In an instant it will collapse and come crashing down.*

Lamentations 1:9
> *She defiled herself with immorality with no thought of the punishment that would follow. Now she lies in the gutter with no one to lift her out.*

It may seem for a time that sin does not have consequences, but consequences always come, sooner or later.

Ezekiel 44:12

They encouraged my people to worship other gods, causing Israel to fall into deep sin. So I have raised my hand and taken an oath that they must bear the consequences for their sins, says the Sovereign LORD.

Micah 2:3

This is what the LORD says: "I will reward your evil with evil; you won't be able to escape!"

God has promised with an oath that those who sin will bear the consequences of what they do.

1 Corinthians 3:13-15

There is going to come a time of testing at the judgment day to see what kind of work each builder has done. Everyone's work will be put through the fire to see whether or not it keeps its value. If the work survives the fire, that builder will receive a reward. But if the work is burned up, the builder will suffer great loss. The builders themselves will be saved, but like someone escaping through a wall of flames.

Some of the consequences of sin will not be felt until the Day of judgment. Even those who have salvation through Jesus Christ will feel the consequences of their sin.

Galatians 6:8

Those who live only to satisfy their own sinful desires will harvest the consequences of decay and death. But those who live to please the Spirit will harvest everlasting life from the Spirit.

Sin always has negative consequences, but the reverse is also true: Living to please God always has positive consequences.

DO WE EVER SUFFER THE CONSEQUENCES OF ANOTHER PERSON'S SIN?

Romans 5:12

> *Adam's sin brought death, so death spread to everyone, for everyone sinned.*

We do suffer the consequences of Adam's sin, but it is also our own sin—we, too, have sinned and deserve the death that he brought.

Isaiah 10:1-2

> *Destruction is certain for the unjust judges, for those who issue unfair laws. They deprive the poor, the widows, and the orphans of justice. Yes, they rob widows and fatherless children!*

The poor, the widows, and the orphans sometimes have to live with the reality of others' sins, but God will make certain that justice is done and that those who sin will bear the consequences of their own injustice.

Ezekiel 18:20

> *The one who sins is the one who dies. The child will not be punished for the parent's sins, and the parent will not be punished for the child's sins. Righteous people will be rewarded for their own goodness, and wicked people will be punished for their own wickedness.*

Ultimately those who sin and those who do good will each receive the consequences of their own actions.

PROMISE FROM GOD:

Romans 6:23

> The wages of sin is death, but the free gift of God is eternal life through Christ Jesus our Lord.

Cooperation

WHY IS IT THAT EVEN THOUGH I LOVE GOD, I FIND IT DIFFICULT TO FOLLOW HIM FAITHFULLY ALL THE TIME?

Jonah 1:1-3

> The LORD gave this message to Jonah. . . . "Get up and go to the great city of Nineveh! Announce my judgment against it because I have seen how wicked its people are." But Jonah got up and went in the opposite direction.

Sometimes fear keeps us from following God—fear of failure, fear of being ridiculed for our faith, fear of persecution. When God calls you to a specific task, don't let fear get in the way.

Romans 7:15

> I don't understand myself at all, for I really want to do what is right, but I don't do it. Instead, I do the very thing I hate.

Even Paul found himself struggling with his old sinful nature. At such times we have the power of the Holy Spirit to help us do what is right.

How do I respond when I have difficulty cooperating with others?

Exodus 17:12-13

> Moses' arms finally became too tired to hold up the staff any longer. So Aaron and Hur found a stone for him to sit on. Then they stood on each side, holding up his hands until sunset. As a result, Joshua and his troops were able to crush the army of Amalek.

Moses and Aaron did not always see eye to eye, but in this instance of cooperation, the result was a decisive win for the Israelites. When we do cooperate together, God can accomplish remarkable things through us.

Proverbs 27:17

> As iron sharpens iron, a friend sharpens a friend.

Disagreement can produce a positive result—it can introduce new ideas that may challenge and stimulate our thinking.

1 Corinthians 1:10

> Dear brothers and sisters, I appeal to you by the authority of the Lord Jesus Christ to stop arguing among yourselves. Let there be real harmony so there won't be divisions in the church. I plead with you to be of one mind, united in thought and purpose.

Loving confrontation is different from argumentativeness. Conflict is inevitable; when it arises, true cooperation seeks the highest good for all.

PROMISE FROM GOD:

Psalm 133:1

> *How wonderful it is, how pleasant, when brothers live together in harmony!*

Courage

WHERE DO I GET THE COURAGE TO GO ON WHEN LIFE SEEMS TOO HARD OR OBSTACLES SEEM TOO BIG?

Deuteronomy 20:1

> *The LORD your God . . . is with you!*

Psalm 27:1

> *The LORD is my light and my salvation—so why should I be afraid?*

Isaiah 41:10

> *Don't be afraid, for I am with you. Do not be dismayed, for I am your God. I will strengthen you. I will help you. I will uphold you with my victorious right hand.*

Joshua 1:9

> *Be strong and courageous! Do not be afraid or discouraged. For the LORD your God is with you wherever you go.*

True courage comes from God, from understanding that he is stronger than our mightiest foes and wants to use his strength to help us.

How do I find the courage to face change?
Genesis 46:3
> *Do not be afraid to go down to Egypt, for I will see to it that you become a great nation there.*

Change may be part of God's plan for us. If so, we can trust God to take care of us through the changes.

Exodus 4:13
> *But Moses again pleaded, "Lord, please! Send someone else."*

Fear is normal. Being paralyzed by fear, however, can be an indication that you doubt God's ability to care for you in the face of change.

2 Samuel 4:1
> *When Ishbosheth heard about Abner's death at Hebron, he lost all courage, and his people were paralyzed with fear.*

If you take all of your courage from another person, you will be left with nothing when that person is gone. If you trust in God, you will have the strength to go on even when circumstances collapse around you.

How do I find the courage to admit my mistakes?
2 Samuel 12:13
> *Then David confessed to Nathan, "I have sinned against the LORD." Nathan replied, "Yes, but the LORD has forgiven you."*

Admitting our mistakes and sins opens the door to forgiveness and helps restore relationships.

ARE THERE CONSEQUENCES TO A LACK OF COURAGE?

Luke 23:23-24

Their voices prevailed. So Pilate sentenced Jesus to die as they demanded.

Standing up for what is right can get you into trouble from corrupt people. Failing to stand up for what is right can get you into trouble with God.

PROMISE FROM GOD:

Joshua 1:9

I command you—be strong and courageous! Do not be afraid or discouraged. For the LORD your God is with you wherever you go.

Crisis

WHAT ARE SOME POSSIBLE REASONS FOR CRISIS IN MY LIFE?

Jonah 1:4, 12-15

As the ship was sailing along, suddenly the LORD flung a powerful wind over the sea, causing a violent storm that threatened to send them to the bottom. . . . "Throw me into the sea," Jonah said, "and it will become calm again. For I know that this terrible storm is all my fault." . . . Then they cried out to the LORD, Jonah's God. "O LORD," they pleaded, "don't make us die for this man's sin. And don't hold us responsible for his death, because it isn't our fault. O LORD, you have sent this storm upon him for your own good reasons." Then the sailors picked Jonah up and threw him into the raging sea, and the storm stopped at once!

Jonah was in crisis for running away from God, but the sailors were in crisis too because of someone else's sin! Your sin can place others in crisis. And your crisis may be the result of someone else's sin.

Jeremiah 16:10-12

When you tell the people all these things, they will ask, "Why has the LORD decreed such terrible things against us? What have we done to deserve such treatment? What is our sin against the LORD our God?" Tell them that this is the LORD's reply: It is because your ancestors were unfaithful to me. They worshiped other gods and served them. They abandoned me. They did not keep my law. And you are even worse than your ancestors! You stubbornly follow your own evil desires and refuse to listen to me.

The consequences of sin spread to innocent people and are carried along from generation to generation.

Proverbs 27:12

A prudent person foresees the danger ahead and takes precautions. The simpleton goes blindly on and suffers the consequences.

Sometime crisis comes because we have made unwise decisions.

2 Corinthians 4:11

Yes, we live under constant danger of death because we serve Jesus, so that the life of Jesus will be obvious in our dying bodies.

Sometimes crisis comes because we serve Jesus, and serving Jesus can bring persecution.

WHAT ARE SOME BENEFITS OF TIMES OF CRISIS?

Jonah 1:16

> *The sailors were awestruck by the LORD's great power, and they offered him a sacrifice and vowed to serve him.*

Sometimes a crisis helps people see God more clearly.

Philippians 1:12-14

> *I want you to know, dear brothers and sisters, that everything that has happened to me here has helped to spread the Good News. For everyone here, including all the soldiers in the palace guard, knows that I am in chains because of Christ. And because of my imprisonment, many of the Christians here have gained confidence and become more bold in telling others about Christ.*

How we respond to times of crisis can influence what others think about Christ.

Romans 5:3-4

> *We can rejoice, too, when we run into problems and trials, for we know that they are good for us—they help us learn to endure. And endurance develops strength of character in us, and character strengthens our confident expectation of salvation.*

Times of crisis have the potential to strengthen our character.

2 Corinthians 12:10

> *Since I know it is all for Christ's good, I am quite content with my weaknesses and with insults, hardships, persecutions, and calamities. For when I am weak, then I am strong.*

Times of crisis show us that we cannot always rely on our own strength to see us through. God's strength is what we need. Spiritual strength can grow from physical weakness.

1 Peter 1:6-7

> *Be truly glad! There is wonderful joy ahead, even though it is necessary for you to endure many trials for a while. These trials are only to test your faith, to show that it is strong and pure.*

Times of crisis test our faith.

1 Peter 4:12-14

> *Dear friends, don't be surprised at the fiery trials you are going through, as if something strange were happening to you. Instead, be very glad— because these trials will make you partners with Christ in his suffering, and afterward you will have the wonderful joy of sharing his glory when it is displayed to all the world. Be happy if you are insulted for being a Christian, for then the glorious Spirit of God will come upon you.*

Times of crisis help us identify with the suffering that Jesus endured for our sake.

HOW SHOULD I RESPOND TO CRISIS?

Jonah 2:1-2

> *Then Jonah prayed to the LORD his God from inside the fish.*

> He said, "I cried out to the LORD in my great trouble, and he answered me. I called to you from the world of the dead, and LORD, you heard me!"

Psalm 130:1-2

> From the depths of despair, O LORD, I call for your help. Hear my cry, O Lord. Pay attention to my prayer.

When we reach the end of our rope, we must call upon the Lord, for our weaknesses are times for his strength; our crises are his opportunities.

Psalm 57:1

> Have mercy on me, O God, have mercy! I look to you for protection. I will hide beneath the shadow of your wings until this violent storm is past.

When a crisis leaves us vulnerable and exposed, we should seek the merciful protective covering of the Lord himself.

Psalm 28:7

> The LORD is my strength, my shield from every danger. I trust in him with all my heart. He helps me, and my heart is filled with joy. I burst out in songs of thanksgiving.

A crisis may leave us wondering, Whom can I trust? Crisis should leave us assured that we can always trust the Lord. That is cause for praise and thanksgiving.

Psalm 119:143

> *As pressure and stress bear down on me, I find joy in your commands.*

When crises seek to undermine us, we should look to God's word to undergird us.

WHAT IS GOD'S ADVICE FOR ME IN CRISIS?

Isaiah 30:20-21

> *Though the Lord gave you adversity for food and affliction for drink, he will still be with you to teach you. You will see your teacher with your own eyes, and you will hear a voice say, "This is the way; turn around and walk here."*

John 16:33

> *Here on earth you will have many trials and sorrows. But take heart, because I have overcome the world.*

Matthew 5:11-12

> *God blesses you when you are mocked and persecuted and lied about because you are my followers. Be happy about it! Be very glad! For a great reward awaits you in heaven. And remember, the ancient prophets were persecuted, too.*

God does not say he will always prevent crisis in our life—we live in a sinful world where terrible things happen. But God does promise always to be with us, helping us through any crisis.

WHERE IS GOD IN MY TIME OF CRISIS?

Jonah 1:17

> *The LORD had arranged for a great fish to swallow Jonah. And Jonah was inside the fish for three days and three nights.*

Jonah 2.6

> I sank down to the very roots of the mountains. I was locked out of life and imprisoned in the land of the dead. But you, O LORD my God, have snatched me from the yawning jaws of death!

Psalm 40.2

> He lifted me out of the pit of despair, out of the mud and the mire. He set my feet on solid ground and steadied me as I walked along.

Psalm 46.1-2

> God is our refuge and strength, always ready to help in times of trouble. So we will not fear.

Psalm 69.33

> For the LORD hears the cries of his needy ones; he does not despise his people who are oppressed.

Romans 8.35

> Can anything ever separate us from Christ's love? Does it mean he no longer loves us if we have trouble or calamity, or are persecuted, or are hungry or cold or in danger or threatened with death?

We need not pray for the Lord to be with us in times of crisis. He is already with us. Instead we need to pray that we might recognize his presence and then depend on him for help.

PROMISE FROM GOD:

John 16.33

> I have told you all this so that you may have peace in me. Here on earth you will have many trials and sorrows. But take heart, because I have overcome the world.

Criticism

HOW SHOULD I RESPOND TO CRITICISM? HOW DO I EVALUATE WHETHER CRITICISM IS CONSTRUCTIVE OR DESTRUCTIVE?

Proverbs 12.16-18

A wise person stays calm when insulted. An honest witness tells the truth; a false witness tells lies. Some people make cutting remarks, but the words of the wise bring healing.

If you are criticized, stay calm, and don't lash back. Evaluate whether the criticism is coming from a person with a reputation for telling the truth or telling lies. Ask yourself if the criticism is meant to heal or to hurt.

Ecclesiastes 7.5

It is better to be criticized by a wise person than to be praised by a fool!

Measure criticism according to the character of the person who is giving it.

1 Corinthians 4.4-5

My conscience is clear, but that isn't what matters. It is the Lord himself who will examine me and decide.

Always work to maintain a clear conscience by being honest and trustworthy. This allows you to shrug off criticism that you know is unjustified.

1 Peter 4:14

> *Be happy if you are insulted for being a Christian, for then the glorious Spirit of God will come upon you.*

Consider it a privilege to be criticized for your faith in God. God has special blessings for those who patiently endure this kind of criticism.

How can I benefit from constructive criticism?

Proverbs 15:31

> *If you listen to constructive criticism, you will be at home among the wise.*

We shortchange ourselves when we reject truthful constructive criticism. Sometimes it is painful to hear the truth, but it is worse to ignore it and move into the future without improvement.

Should we be careful about criticizing others?

Romans 14:10

> *Why do you condemn another Christian? . . . Remember, each of us will stand personally before the judgment seat of God.*

James 4:11

> *If you criticize each other and condemn each other, then you are criticizing and condemning God's law.*

Constructive criticism should always be a welcome and whole-some gift if given in a spirit of love. But we have no right to give deprecating criticism of another, for that is trying to be a judge over that person, and God alone is our judge.

HOW DO WE PREVENT UNJUST CRITICISM AGAINST US?

Romans 14:18

If you serve Christ with this attitude, you will please God. And other people will approve of you too.

Matthew 7:1

Stop judging others, and you will not be judged.

We can usually avoid others' criticisms by avoiding words and actions that warrant criticism. But we must recognize that some people will criticize us simply because we are followers of God.

HOW DO WE ADMINISTER CRITICISM WHEN WE FEEL IT MUST BE GIVEN?

John 8:7

Let those who have never sinned throw the first stones!

Romans 2:1

When you say they are wicked and should be punished, you are condemning yourself, for you do these very same things.

Before criticizing another, take an inventory of your own sins and shortcomings so that you can approach the person with understanding and humility.

1 Corinthians 13:5
> *Love does not demand its own way. Love is not irritable, and it keeps no record of when it has been wronged.*

Constructive criticism must always be offered in love, motivated by a desire to build up.

PROMISE FROM GOD:

1 Peter 4:14
> *Be happy if you are insulted for being a Christian, for then the glorious Spirit of God will come upon you.*

Cults

WHAT IS A CULT?

Judges 2:19
> *When the judge died, the people returned to their corrupt ways, behaving worse than those who had lived before them. They followed other gods, worshiping and bowing down to them. And they refused to give up their evil practices and stubborn ways.*

A cult is a group of people who offer their wholehearted worship and devotion to anything or anyone other than the God of the Bible. Cults tend to be isolationist and very possessive, to practice bizarre rituals, and to follow a religious system instituted by a person with a very engaging personality. Cults institute a religious system that is contrary to what God has established in the Bible.

How can I tell if an organization is a cult?

Matthew 7:15-17

> *Beware of false prophets who come disguised as harmless sheep,
> but are really wolves that will tear you apart. You can detect
> them by the way they act, just as you can identify a tree by its
> fruit. You don't pick grapes from thornbushes, or figs from
> thistles. A healthy tree produces good fruit, and an unhealthy
> tree produces bad fruit.*

You must compare the teachings of any religious group with the
teachings in the Bible. That's why it is so important to know
your Bible. If the teachings of a religious group are contrary to
what is found in God's Word, and if they tell you that their way
is the only way to true peace and happiness, then you may be
dealing with a cult.

Romans 10:9

> *If you confess with your mouth that Jesus is Lord and believe in
> your heart that God raised him from the dead, you will be
> saved.*

Cults do not teach that faith in Jesus Christ as Savior and
forgiveness of sins through him alone is the only way to heaven.

Daniel 6:7

> *We administrators, prefects, princes, advisers, and other officials
> have unanimously agreed that Your Majesty should make a law
> that will be strictly enforced. Give orders that for the next thirty
> days anyone who prays to anyone, divine or human—except to
> Your Majesty—will be thrown to the lions.*

There are many danger signs that can warn you that a group is a cult. Jesus said that you can tell a man's heart by his actions. Although Daniel wasn't facing a cult, he was facing a group that was trying to divert his worship away from God. Cults will try to do the same thing.

CAN GOD FORGIVE ME FOR HAVING BEEN INVOLVED IN A CULT?

1 John 1:9

> *If we confess our sins to him, he is faithful and just to forgive us and to cleanse us from every wrong.*

Isaiah 44:22

> *I have swept away your sins like the morning mists. I have scattered your offenses like the clouds. Oh, return to me, for I have paid the price to set you free.*

God longs for all people to turn to him. He forgives any sin.

Dating

IS THERE A RIGHT WAY AND A WRONG WAY TO DATE?

Deuteronomy 7:3-4

> *Do not intermarry with them, and don't let your daughters and sons marry their sons and daughters. They will lead your young people away from me to worship other gods.*

2 Corinthians 6.14

> *Don't team up with those who are unbelievers. How can goodness be a partner with wickedness? How can light live with darkness?*

God repeatedly warns against marrying someone who is not a Christian. The Bible says that by doing so you set yourself up for being drawn away from God. Dating an unbeliever can lead to the kind of marriage God warns against.

1 Thessalonians 4.3-5

> *God wants you to be holy, so you should keep clear of all sexual sin. Then each of you will control your body and live in holiness and honor—not in lustful passion.*

You should guard yourself against physical intimacy in a dating relationship. Such intimacy is reserved only for marriage because it is a picture of the purity and devotion we should reserve for God in our worship.

WHAT DOES GOD SAY MY BOUNDARIES SHOULD BE IN MY DATING RELATIONSHIP?

Hebrews 13.18

> *Pray for us, for our conscience is clear and we want to live honorably in everything we do.*

We are called to live a pure and honorable life and to maintain a clear conscience. The best way to maintain purity, honor, and a clear conscience is to save physical intimacy and words of love until a committed lifelong relationship is established.

HOW CAN I HANDLE SOMEONE WHO IS PUSHING ME TOWARD A PHYSICAL RELATIONSHIP?

1 Timothy 4:12

> *Don't let anyone think less of you because you are young. Be an*
> *example to all believers in what you teach, in the way you live,*
> *in your love, your faith, and your purity.*

It is better to stay pure than to give in to pressure. If the one you
are dating is really a friend who is caring and concerned for what's
best for you, that person will honor and respect your desire for
purity before marriage.

PROMISE FROM GOD:

Hebrews 13:4

> *Give honor to marriage, and remain faithful to one another in*
> *marriage. God will surely judge people who are immoral and*
> *those who commit adultery.*

Decisions

WHAT MUST I DO TO MAKE GOOD DECISIONS?

Psalm 25:4

> *Show me the path where I should walk, O LORD; point out the*
> *right road for me to follow.*

Follow God's direction.

Luke 6:12-13

> One day soon afterward Jesus went to a mountain to pray, and he prayed to God all night. At daybreak he called together all of his disciples and chose twelve of them to be apostles.

Saturate your life with prayer.

Romans 2:18

> Yes, you know what he wants; you know right from wrong because you have been taught his law.

Consult God's word for God's wisdom.

Proverbs 12:15

> Fools think they need no advice, but the wise listen to others.

Psalm 37:30

> The godly offer good counsel; they know right from wrong.

Listen to godly counsel.

Proverbs 18:15

> Intelligent people are always open to new ideas. In fact, they look for them.

Be open to good advice.

HOW DOES GOD GUIDE OUR DECISION MAKING?

Psalm 25:12

> Who are those who fear the LORD? He will show them the path they should choose.

Proverbs 4:5

> *Learn to be wise, and develop good judgment. Don't forget or*
> *turn away from my words.*

Philippians 2:13

> *God is working in you, giving you the desire to obey him and*
> *the power to do what pleases him.*

We should pray for God to give us the desire to obey him and seek his guidance. When we obey, he will guide.

HOW CAN I MAKE A WISE DECISION IN A DIFFICULT SITUATION?

Daniel 3:14-18

> *Nebuchadnezzar said to them, "Is it true, Shadrach, Meshach,*
> *and Abednego, that you refuse to serve my gods or to worship the*
> *gold statue I have set up? I will give you one more chance. If you*
> *bow down and worship the statue I have made when you hear*
> *the sound of the musical instruments, all will be well. But if you*
> *refuse, you will be thrown immediately into the blazing*
> *furnace. What god will be able to rescue you from my power*
> *then?" Shadrach, Meshach, and Abednego replied, "O*
> *Nebuchadnezzar, we do not need to defend ourselves before you.*
> *If we are thrown into the blazing furnace, the God whom we*
> *serve is able to save us. He will rescue us from your power, Your*
> *Majesty. But even if he doesn't, Your Majesty can be sure that*
> *we will never serve your gods or worship the gold statue you*
> *have set up."*

Isaiah 51:7

> *Listen to me, you who know right from wrong and cherish my*
> *law in your hearts. Do not be afraid of people's scorn or their*
> *slanderous talk.*

From a short-term perspective, the right decision may not seem like the safest one. Trust God—he will always do what is right from an eternal perspective, even though it may seem harmful to you at the time.

WHAT IS THE DANGER OF INDECISION?

Isaiah 42:20

> You see and understand what is right but refuse to act on it. You hear, but you don't really listen.

James 1:5-8

> If you need wisdom—if you want to know what God wants you to do—ask him, and he will gladly tell you. . . . But when you ask him, be sure that you really expect him to answer, for a doubtful mind is as unsettled as a wave of the sea that is driven and tossed by the wind. People like that should not expect to receive anything from the Lord. They can't make up their minds. They waver back and forth in everything they do.

Indecision is really a decision not to make a decision. Indecision regarding matters of faith can slowly but persistently draw us away from God.

HOW DO I KNOW IF I'VE MADE A GOOD DECISION?

2 Timothy 3:16

> All Scripture is inspired by God and is useful to teach us what is true and to make us realize what is wrong in our lives. It straightens us out and teaches us to do what is right.

Psalm 79:9

> Help us, O God of our salvation! Help us for the honor of your name. Oh, save us and forgive our sins for the sake of your name.

Galatians 5:22-23

> *When the Holy Spirit controls our lives, he will produce this kind of fruit in us: love, joy, peace, patience, kindness, goodness, faithfulness, gentleness, and self-control. Here there is no conflict with the law.*

You always make the right decision when you follow the commands God has given in the Bible. Also, always check your motives—are you deciding based on what *you* want or on what is best for others? Are you making a decision that is helping others or hurting them?

HOW IS MY CHARACTER REVEALED IN MY DECISIONS?

Genesis 13:10-11

> *Lot took a long look at the fertile plains of the Jordan Valley in the direction of Zoar. The whole area was well watered everywhere, like the garden of the LORD or the beautiful land of Egypt. (This was before the LORD had destroyed Sodom and Gomorrah.) Lot chose that land for himself—the Jordan Valley to the east of them. He went there with his flocks and servants and parted company with his uncle Abram.*

Proverbs 14:2

> *Those who follow the right path fear the LORD; those who take the wrong path despise him.*

Your decisions determine your actions, and your actions show what is in your heart.

PROMISE FROM GOD:

Proverbs 3:6

> *Seek his will in all you do, and he will direct your paths.*

Depression

WHAT CAUSES DEPRESSION?

1 Samuel 16:14

> *Now the Spirit of the LORD had left Saul, and the LORD sent a tormenting spirit that filled him with depression and fear.*

If you depart from the Lord and then he departs from you, depression can move easily into the vacant room in your heart.

Job 30:16

> *Now my heart is broken. Depression haunts my days.*

A broken heart is ripe for depression.

Ecclesiastes 4:8

> *This is the case of a man who is all alone, without a child or a brother, yet who works hard to gain as much wealth as he can. But then he asks himself, "Who am I working for? Why am I giving up so much pleasure now?" It is all so meaningless and depressing.*

If you spend your life pursuing meaningless things, you are bound to get depressed as you realize that what you are doing has little lasting value.

Proverbs 13:12

> *Hope deferred makes the heart sick, but when dreams come true, there is life and joy.*

A heart without hope is a heart ripe for depression.

HOW SHOULD I HANDLE DEPRESSION?

Psalm 143:7

> *Come quickly, LORD, and answer me, for my depression deepens. Don't turn away from me, or I will die.*

The Lord's strong presence in our life is the best cure for depression. But with the Lord's help, we may also seek the best medical help and ask him to use it to heal us.

HOW DOES GOD BRING HEALING TO THOSE WHO ARE DEPRESSED?

Psalm 10:17

> *LORD, you know the hopes of the helpless. Surely you will listen to their cries and comfort them.*

Psalm 23:4

> *Even when I walk through the dark valley of death, I will not be afraid, for you are close beside me. Your rod and your staff protect and comfort me.*

Psalm 34:18

> *The LORD is close to the brokenhearted; he rescues those who are crushed in spirit.*

Psalm 147:3

> *He heals the brokenhearted, binding up their wounds.*

Matthew 5:4

> *God blesses those who mourn, for they will be comforted.*

The power of the Lord's presence, coupled with the sensitivity of his listening ear, can bring healing and comfort.

CAN ANY GOOD COME OUT OF DEPRESSION?

Psalm 126:5

> *Those who plant in tears will harvest with shouts of joy.*

Nehemiah 8:10

> *Don't be dejected and sad, for the joy of the LORD is your strength!*

2 Corinthians 12:9

> *My power works best in your weakness.*

When we are weak, we may be more receptive to the Lord's strength. When God works through our weakness, we know it is his work and not ours.

HOW CAN I HELP PEOPLE WHO ARE DEPRESSED?

2 Corinthians 1:4

> *He comforts us in all our troubles so that we can comfort others. When others are troubled, we will be able to give them the same comfort God has given us.*

Romans 12:15

> *When others are happy, be happy with them. If they are sad, share their sorrow.*

Proverbs 25:20

> *Singing cheerful songs to a person whose heart is heavy is as bad as stealing someone's jacket in cold weather or rubbing salt in a wound.*

The best way to help depressed people is to comfort them.

PROMISE FROM GOD:
Matthew 11:28

> *Then Jesus said, "Come to me, all of you who are weary and carry heavy burdens, and I will give you rest."*

Distractions

WHAT IS THE DANGER IN DISTRACTIONS?
Luke 9:62

> *But Jesus told him, "Anyone who puts a hand to the plow and then looks back is not fit for the Kingdom of God."*

Matthew 14:28-31

> *Then Peter called to him, "Lord, if it's really you, tell me to come to you by walking on water." "All right, come," Jesus said. So Peter went over the side of the boat and walked on the water toward Jesus. But when he looked around at the high waves, he was terrified and began to sink. "Save me, Lord!" he shouted. Instantly Jesus reached out his hand and grabbed him. "You don't have much faith," Jesus said. "Why did you doubt me?"*

Distractions take our focus off of Jesus. We can be in the middle of doing great things, but if we take our eyes off of Jesus, we can begin to sink!

How can God use distractions?

Exodus 3:1-4

> One day Moses was tending the flock of his father-in-law,
> Jethro. . . . Suddenly, the angel of the LORD appeared to him as
> a blazing fire in a bush. Moses was amazed because the bush
> was engulfed in flames, but it didn't burn up. . . . "Why isn't
> that bush burning up? I must go over to see this." When the
> LORD saw that he had caught Moses' attention, God called to
> him from the bush.

Moses was out on an ordinary day doing his ordinary job! God
used the bush, a definite distraction, to get Moses' attention.

Acts 9:3-4

> As [Saul] was nearing Damascus on this mission, a brilliant
> light from heaven suddenly beamed down upon him! He fell to
> the ground and heard a voice saying to him, "Saul! Saul! Why
> are you persecuting me?"

God can refocus our sights on *his* ways, distracting us from *our*
ways. Paul was on his mission to persecute Christians when God
got his attention with a distraction that was even harder to
ignore than Moses' bush.

How do I deal with distractions?

Mark 10:17

> As he was starting out on a trip, a man came running up to
> Jesus, knelt down, and asked, "Good Teacher, what should I do
> to get eternal life?"

Matthew 19:13-15

> *Some children were brought to Jesus so he could lay his hands on them and pray for them. The disciples told them not to bother him. But Jesus said, "Let the children come to me. Don't stop them! For the Kingdom of Heaven belongs to such as these." And he put his hands on their heads and blessed them before he left.*

Distractions happened all the time in Jesus' ministry. The difference in the way he handled distractions is that he just worked the distractions right into the main focus of his life! In other words, Jesus didn't see them as distractions, just as opportunities to save the lost!

Acts 16:29-32

> *Trembling with fear, the jailer called for lights and ran to the dungeon and fell down before Paul and Silas. He brought them out and asked, "Sirs, what must I do to be saved?" They replied, "Believe on the Lord Jesus and you will be saved, along with your entire household." Then they shared the word of the Lord with him.*

Some of us would have looked at a jail sentence as a definite distraction from our mission for God. Not Paul and Silas! Their mission just continued in the jail cell!

HOW DO WE REMAIN FOCUSED AMID DISTRACTIONS?

Hebrews 12:13

> *Mark out a straight path for your feet. Then those who follow you, though they are weak and lame, will not stumble and fall but will become strong.*

Make clear goals for how you will serve God, and then follow those goals without wavering.

Acts 6:3-4

"Look around among yourselves, brothers, and select seven men who are well respected and are full of the Holy Spirit and wisdom. We will put them in charge of this business. Then we can spend our time in prayer and preaching and teaching the word."

Stay focused on what you do well, and learn to delegate what others can do better.

Psalm 119:157

Many persecute and trouble me, yet I have not swerved from your decrees.

Daniel 6:13

They told the king, "That man Daniel, one of the captives from Judah, is paying no attention to you or your law. He still prays to his God three times a day."

Don't be distracted, even by good things, if they take you away from what you know is right.

Philippians 3:13

No, dear brothers and sisters, I am still not all I should be, but I am focusing all my energies on this one thing: Forgetting the past and looking forward to what lies ahead.

Don't let the past drag you down; focus your energies on what you can do for God and others now and in the future.

Psalm 66:9

> *Our lives are in his hands, and he keeps our feet from stumbling.*

Keep your eyes fixed on the Lord.

Proverbs 4:12

> *If you live a life guided by wisdom, you won't limp or stumble as you run.*

Constantly seek wisdom.

PROMISE FROM GOD:

Hebrews 12:13

> *Mark out a straight path for your feet. Then those who follow you, though they are weak and lame, will not stumble and fall but will become strong.*

Doubt

SOMETIMES I FIND MYSELF DOUBTING GOD AND MY FAITH, AND I FEEL ASHAMED. WHAT CAN I DO?

Psalm 94:19

> *When doubts filled my mind, your comfort gave me renewed hope and cheer.*

Matthew 14:31

> *Instantly Jesus reached out his hand and grabbed him. "You don't have much faith," Jesus said. "Why did you doubt me?"*

Both David and Peter struggled with doubt. Both men recognized their weakness and humbled themselves before God, and God used them. God doesn't mind doubt as long as we are seeking him for help with our doubt!

Psalm 95:9

> *There your ancestors tried my patience; they courted my wrath though they had seen my many miracles.*

God gives us plenty of evidence to believe in him. Doubt comes when we ignore all the evidence. And when doubt turns to disbelief, we are in danger of ignoring God altogether.

John 20:27

> *"Don't be faithless any longer. Believe!"*

Doubt can be healthy or destructive, depending on how we use it. Use your doubts to learn about God and to make your faith stronger.

ARE THERE THINGS WE SHOULD NEVER DOUBT?

Ephesians 1:14

> *The Spirit is God's guarantee that he will give us everything he promised and that he has purchased us to be his own people.*

Hebrews 13:5

> *God has said, "I will never fail you. I will never forsake you."*

We should never doubt God's promise of salvation. God has promised that as Christians, we will live forever with him in heaven. Satan can never snatch us away from our eternal life with God.

2 Corinthians 6:2
> *Indeed, God is ready to help you right now.*

We should never doubt God's desire or ability to help us.

PROMISE FROM GOD:
Hebrews 13:5
> *God has said, "I will never fail you. I will never forsake you."*

Drinking

WHEN DOES DRINKING BECOME WRONG?
Ephesians 5:18
> *Don't be drunk with wine, because that will ruin your life. Instead, let the Holy Spirit fill and control you.*

Exodus 32:6
> *The people got up early the next morning to sacrifice burnt offerings and peace offerings. After this, they celebrated with feasting and drinking, and indulged themselves in pagan revelry.*

Drinking becomes wrong when it leads to drunkenness, when it controls our actions, or when it causes us to disobey and dishonor God. (For minors, this includes drinking at any time.)

I'M ADDICTED TO DRINKING. CAN GOD HELP ME?
2 Corinthians 5:17

> What this means is that those who become Christians become new persons. They are not the same anymore, for the old life is gone. A new life has begun!

God can and will help anyone who is trapped by an addiction if that person will confess the sin and call upon God to help.

PROMISE FROM GOD:
1 Corinthians 10:13

> Remember that the temptations that come into your life are no different from what others experience. And God is faithful. He will keep the temptation from becoming so strong that you can't stand up against it. When you are tempted, he will show you a way out so that you will not give in to it.

Drugs

WHAT DOES THE BIBLE SAY ABOUT DRUGS?

1 Corinthians 6:12-13

You may say, "I am allowed to do anything." But I reply, "Not everything is good for you." And even though "I am allowed to do anything," I must not become a slave to anything. . . . Our bodies . . . were made for the Lord, and the Lord cares about our bodies.

1 Corinthians 6:19-20

Don't you know that your body is the temple of the Holy Spirit, who lives in you and was given to you by God? You do not belong to yourself, for God bought you with a high price. So you must honor God with your body.

1 Corinthians 10:31

Whatever you eat or drink or whatever you do, you must do all for the glory of God.

The Bible doesn't talk about drugs as we know of them today, but it does talk very specifically about not putting things into our body that are harmful or that are not glorifying to God. Taking drugs is trying to get a "high"—a feeling of ecstacy and satisfaction that is a cheap substitute for the incredible joy that comes when the Holy Spirit controls our life.

WE ARE TOLD THAT EVERYTHING IS OK IN MODERATION. CAN'T THAT APPLY TO DRUGS, TOO?

2 Peter 2:19

> They promise freedom, but they themselves are slaves to sin and corruption. For you are a slave to whatever controls you.

Whatever has control over you is your master. If God is your master, he will raise you up and encourage you, but drugs will only tear you down and make you a slave to their addictive power.

PROMISE FROM GOD:

Romans 8:5

> Those who are dominated by the sinful nature think about sinful things, but those who are controlled by the Holy Spirit think about things that please the Spirit.

Embarrassment

I SOMETIMES LOSE MY TEMPER WHEN I'M EMBARRASSED—IS THAT WRONG?

Numbers 22:29

> "You have made me look like a fool!" Balaam shouted.

Embarrassment is often the result of wounded pride. When we are embarrassed, we should ask if we need to learn something.

Nehemiah 4:4

> *Then I prayed, "Hear us, O our God, for we are being mocked."*

Nehemiah's response to being mocked was not anger but renewed prayer and focus on his task.

HOW SHOULD A CHRISTIAN HANDLE EMBARRASSING SITUATIONS?

Matthew 1:19

> *Joseph, her fiancé, being a just man, decided to break the engagement quietly, so as not to disgrace her publicly.*

Even when his engagement and personal reputation were on the line, Joseph was careful not to humiliate Mary publicly.

Matthew 14:9

> *The king was sorry, but because of his oath and because he didn't want to back down in front of his guests, he issued the necessary orders.*

We must not allow the threat of embarrassment to pressure us into doing what we know is sin.

SOMETIMES MY FRIENDS MAKE FUN OF MY CHRISTIAN FAITH.

Mark 8:38

> *If a person is ashamed of me and my message in these adulterous and sinful days, I, the Son of Man, will be ashamed of that person when I return.*

We never have to be ashamed or embarrassed about Jesus.

Romans 1:16

I am not ashamed of this Good News about Christ.

Paul was not ashamed of the Good News, which alone holds the power to save souls for all eternity.

2 Timothy 1:8

You must never be ashamed to tell others about our Lord.

Believers should never be embarrassed to tell others about their faith in Christ.

What does the Bible say about the environment and our responsibility for it?

Genesis 1:28

God blessed them and told them, "Multiply and fill the earth and subdue it. Be masters over the fish and birds and all the animals."

Human beings were created to share responsibility for the earth by being good stewards of the environment.

Genesis 2:15

The LORD God placed the man in the Garden of Eden to tend and care for it.

The first assignment God gave to Adam was to tend and care for his environment.

Deuteronomy 20:19

> *When you are besieging a town and the war drags on, do not destroy the trees. . . . They are not enemies that need to be attacked!*

Even in a time of war, God is concerned that the environment not be needlessly destroyed.

Leviticus 25:5

> *The land is to have a year of total rest.*

God's instructions for the people of Israel to let the farmland rest every seventh year allowed for the conservation of good, productive land.

Psalm 96:12-13

> *Let the fields and their crops burst forth with joy! Let the trees of the forest rustle with praise before the LORD!*

God created nature to proclaim his glory. We should do what we can to preserve this testimony for God.

PROMISE FROM GOD:

Psalm 19:1-4

> *The heavens tell of the glory of God. The skies display his marvelous craftsmanship. Day after day they continue to speak; night after night they make him known . . . yet their message has gone out to all the earth, and their words to all the world.*

Euthanasia

WHY IS EUTHANASIA WRONG?

Psalm 119:73

You made me; you created me. Now give me the sense to follow your commands.

Exodus 20:13

Do not murder.

God created each one of us uniquely. It is he who breathed life into us and he alone who has the right to decide when our life should end. Euthanasia is a direct violation of God's command—it is murder in the cloak of supposed compassion.

DON'T I HAVE THE FINAL SAY OVER WHAT HAPPENS TO MY BODY?

1 Corinthians 6:12-13

You may say, "I am allowed to do anything." But I reply, "Not everything is good for you." And even though "I am allowed to do anything," I must not become a slave to anything. . . . But our bodies were . . . made for the Lord, and the Lord cares about our bodies.

1 Corinthians 3:16-17

Don't you realize that all of you together are the temple of God and that the Spirit of God lives in you? God will bring ruin

*upon anyone who ruins this temple. For God's temple is holy,
and you Christians are that temple.*

Our body was made to worship and glorify God. His Holy
Spirit lives in our body. When we do things that are not good
for our body or that destroy our body, we are breaking down the
temple where God dwells.

DOES GOD REALLY HAVE A PLAN FOR OUR LIFE?
Jeremiah 1:5

*I knew you before I formed you in your mother's womb. Before
you were born I set you apart and appointed you as my
spokesman to the world.*

God has a perfect plan for each of our lives, which includes
being his spokesmen to the world. We must not shortchange
ourselves and God by prematurely ending our own or another's
life.

PROMISE FROM GOD:
Jeremiah 29:11

*"I know the plans I have for you," says the LORD. "They are
plans for good and not for disaster, to give you a future and a
hope."*

Evil

WHY DO PEOPLE OFTEN SEEM TO GET AWAY WITH EVIL?

Jeremiah 12:1-2

> *Why are the wicked so prosperous? Why are evil people so*
> *happy? You have planted them, and they have taken root and*
> *prospered. Your name is on their lips, but in their hearts they*
> *give you no credit at all.*

Even Jeremiah struggled with the apparent prosperity of evil
people. We must remember that because of sin, life on this
earth is not fair. But at the final judgment, God will settle all
accounts, and everything will be fair for all eternity.

Isaiah 32:7-8

> *The smooth tricks of evil people will be exposed, including all*
> *the lies they use to oppress the poor in the courts. But good*
> *people will be generous to others and will be blessed for all*
> *they do.*

It seems that people today can do anything they want and not
only get away with it but also flourish. But God has promised
that in his time everyone will be judged, evil will be exposed,
and the righteous will prevail. God doesn't promise the absence
of evil on this earth. In fact, he warns that evil will be pervasive
and powerful. But God promises to help us stand against evil,

and if we do, we will receive our reward of eternal life with him in heaven, where evil will be no more.

WHY DOES IT SEEM APPEALING TO FLIRT WITH EVIL?

Romans 7:16-17

> *I know perfectly well that what I am doing is wrong, and my bad conscience shows that I agree that the law is good. But I can't help myself, because it is sin inside me that makes me do these evil things.*

Paul recognized that sin causes us to do evil things even when we are focused on doing right. Sin may seem fun; sin may seem beautiful; sin may seem appealing. If it didn't, no one would want to sin. That's why it is so hard to resist.

HOW CAN WE COMBAT EVIL?

Romans 12:21

> *Don't let evil get the best of you, but conquer evil by doing good.*

Romans 13:14

> *Let the Lord Jesus Christ take control of you, and don't think of ways to indulge your evil desires.*

We cannot combat evil on our own. This can happen only when we heed the conviction of the Holy Spirit in our daily life. We combat evil with good. It is one of the most difficult things to do, but it is the most effective.

PROMISE FROM GOD:

Galatians 5:22-23

> When the Holy Spirit controls our lives, he will produce this kind of fruit in us: love, joy, peace, patience, kindness, goodness, faithfulness, gentleness, and self-control.

Evolution

IF THINGS DID NOT EVOLVE, HOW WERE THE EARTH AND LIFE FORMED?

Genesis 1:1

> In the beginning God created the heavens and the earth.

Genesis 1:25-26

> God made all sorts of wild animals, livestock, and small animals, each able to reproduce more of its own kind. And God saw that it was good. Then God said, "Let us make people in our image, to be like ourselves. They will be masters over all life—the fish in the sea, the birds in the sky, and all the livestock, wild animals, and small animals."

The Bible clearly states that God made the heavens, the earth, and all that inhabits it. The Bible doesn't say much about how he did it, but the fact is that God did it.

Excuses

WHERE IS THE FIRST EXCUSE IN THE BIBLE?

Genesis 3:12

> *It was the woman you gave me who brought me the fruit, and I ate it.*

Adam made the first excuse. He blamed Eve, and indirectly he blamed God for giving her to him. Then Eve blamed the serpent. Both tried to excuse their action by blaming someone else.

WHAT ARE SOME EXAMPLES OF OTHER PEOPLE WHO HAD POOR EXCUSES?

Genesis 16:5

> *Then Sarai said to Abram, "It's all your fault!"*

Sarai (Sarah) couldn't have children, so she gave her slave to Abram in order to have a child through her. Later Sarah had second thoughts and blamed Abram for the whole thing.

Exodus 32:24

> *When they brought them to me, I threw them into the fire—and out came this calf!*

Aaron's lame excuse for making an idol—something expressly condemned by God—was that it just happened! How often we do the same thing, blaming our sin on circumstances beyond our control. But we are completely accountable for *all* our actions (Rom. 14:12; Rev. 20:12).

1 Samuel 15:15

> "It's true that the army spared the best of the sheep and cattle," Saul admitted. "But they are going to sacrifice them to the LORD your God. We have destroyed everything else."

Saul tried to justify his sinful actions with one excuse after another. Finally he ran out of excuses and lost his kingdom (1 Sam. 15:26).

Luke 22:60

> Peter said, "Man, I don't know what you are talking about."

Peter wanted to save his life or, at least, avoid the ridicule of being associated with Jesus.

CAN WE EVER EXCUSE OURSELVES FROM GOD'S WORK BECAUSE WE LACK ABILITIES OR RESOURCES?

Exodus 4:10

> Moses pleaded with the LORD, "O Lord, I'm just not a good speaker."

Judges 6:15-16

> "Lord," Gideon replied, "how can I rescue Israel? My clan is the weakest in the whole tribe of Manasseh, and I am the least in my entire family!" The LORD said to him, "I will be with you."

Both Moses and Gideon thought they had a good excuse for not serving God. But the qualifications God looks for are different from what we might expect. He often chooses the least likely people to do his work in order to more effectively demonstrate his power. If you know God has called you to do something, stop trying to excuse yourself. He will give you the help and strength you need to get the job done.

CAN ANYONE BE EXCUSED FOR NOT ACCEPTING THE LORD?

Philippians 2:10-11

> *At the name of Jesus every knee will bow . . . and every tongue will confess that Jesus Christ is Lord.*

We all have excuses for not putting God first—we're too busy, we're not sure how to witness, we'll do it later, we don't know where to start. Do you think those excuses will hold up when we see God face-to-face?

Romans 1:20

> *From the time the world was created, people have seen the earth and sky and all that God made. They can clearly see his invisible qualities—his eternal power and divine nature. So they have no excuse whatsoever for not knowing God.*

Everyone has at least had the testimony of nature, God's work. That alone witnesses to his presence and power. So people who fail to accept the Lord are without excuse.

PROMISE FROM GOD:
1 Peter 1:17

> Remember that the heavenly Father to whom you pray has no favorites when he judges. He will judge or reward you according to what you do. So you must live in reverent fear of him during your time as foreigners here on earth.

Failure

See also **Success**

HOW DO I PREVENT FAILURE IN MY LIFE?
Numbers 14:22

> Not one of these people will ever enter that land. They have seen my glorious presence and the miraculous signs I performed both in Egypt and in the wilderness, but again and again they tested me by refusing to listen.

Hebrews 4:6

> God's rest is there for people to enter. But those who formerly heard the Good News failed to enter because they disobeyed God.

We can prevent failure by listening to God and doing what he says.

Matthew 7:24-27

> *Anyone who listens to my teaching and obeys me is wise, like a person who builds a house on solid rock. Though the rain comes in torrents and the floodwaters rise and the winds beat against that house, it won't collapse, because it is built on rock. But anyone who hears my teaching and ignores it is foolish, like a person who builds a house on sand. When the rains and floods come and the winds beat against that house, it will fall with a mighty crash.*

By listening to Christ and his instructions, we can avoid failure.

1 Chronicles 28:20

> *Be strong and courageous, and do the work. Don't be afraid or discouraged by the size of the task, for the LORD God, my God, is with you.*

When we put our trust completely in God and take courage in his help, we will not fail.

Isaiah 42:23

> *Will not even one of you apply these lessons from the past and see the ruin that awaits you?*

We can avoid failure if we learn from the mistakes of the past.

WHEN I HAVE FAILED, HOW DO I GET PAST IT AND GO ON?

1 Kings 8:33-34

> *If your people Israel are defeated by their enemies because they have sinned against you, and if they turn to you and call on your name and pray to you here in this Temple, then hear from heaven and forgive their sins and return them to this land you gave their ancestors.*

Turning to God in repentance and trust is the best response we can have to our own failure.

Micah 7:8

> Though I fall, I will rise again. Though I sit in darkness, the LORD himself will be my light.

The best response to failure is to get up again, with the hope that comes from faith in God.

PROMISE FROM GOD:

Psalm 37:23-24

> The steps of the godly are directed by the LORD. He delights in every detail of their lives. Though they stumble, they will not fall, for the LORD holds them by the hand.

Faith

WHY SHOULD I HAVE FAITH IN GOD?

Isaiah 25:9

> This is the LORD, in whom we trusted. Let us rejoice in the salvation he brings!

John 5:24

> I assure you, those who listen to my message and believe in God who sent me have eternal life.

Faith is the only way to get to heaven. It is the only doorway to eternal life. If God created eternity, then only through God can we get there.

Hebrews 11:1
> *What is faith? It is the confident assurance that what we hope for is going to happen.*

Faith gives us hope.

HOW DOES FAITH IN GOD AFFECT MY RELATIONSHIP WITH HIM? HOW DOES IT CHANGE THE WAY I LIVE?

Genesis 15:6
> *Abram believed the LORD, and the LORD declared him righteous because of his faith.*

Romans 3:24-25
> *Now God in his gracious kindness declares us not guilty. . . . We are made right with God when we believe that Jesus shed his blood, sacrificing his life for us.*

Sin breaks our relationship with God because it is rebellion against him. A holy God cannot live with unholy people. But when we accept Jesus as Savior and ask him to forgive our sins, this simple act of faith makes us righteous in God's sight.

Isaiah 26:3
> *You will keep in perfect peace all who trust in you.*

Faith in God brings peace of mind and heart because we know that we belong to him and that one day all pain and suffering will end.

Romans 8.5

> *Those who are controlled by the Holy Spirit think about things that please the Spirit.*

1 Corinthians 12.1

> *I will write about the special abilities the Holy Spirit gives to each of us.*

Faith is inviting God's Holy Spirit to live within us. It is not just an act of the mind, but it taps us into the very resources of God so that we have the power to live in an entirely new way. If God himself is living within us, our life should be dramatically changed.

WHEN I'M STRUGGLING AND HAVING DOUBTS, DOES IT MEAN I HAVE LESS FAITH?

2 Peter 1.4-5

> *He has given us all of his rich and wonderful promises. . . . So make every effort to apply the benefits of these promises to your life.*

Genesis 15.8

> *Abram replied, "O Sovereign LORD, how can I be sure that you will give it to me?"*

Matthew 11.2-3

> *John the Baptist . . . sent his disciples to ask Jesus, "Are you really the Messiah we've been waiting for?"*

Many people in the Bible whom we consider to be "pillars of faith" had moments of doubt. The key is to never give up on our faith and to always ask if, over time, our life has been moving closer to or farther away from God. Even during moments of doubt, we must invest the effort and discipline to allow our faith to grow.

PROMISE FROM GOD:
Acts 16:31

> *Believe on the Lord Jesus and you will be saved, along with your entire household.*

Fear

WHAT CAN I DO WHEN I AM OVERCOME WITH FEAR? HOW DO I FIND THE STRENGTH TO GO ON?
Psalm 46:1-2

> *God is our refuge and strength, always ready to help in times of trouble. So we will not fear, even if earthquakes come and the mountains crumble into the sea.*

John 14:27

> *I am leaving you with a gift—peace of mind and heart. . . . So don't be troubled or afraid.*

God promises to comfort us in our fear if we seek him when we are afraid. We have the confident assurance that he is with us in any circumstance.

WHAT DOES IT MEAN TO FEAR GOD?

Psalm 2:11

> *Serve the LORD with reverent fear, and rejoice with trembling.*

Because God is so great and mighty, and because he holds the power of life and death in his hands, we must have a healthy, reverent fear of him. A healthy fear helps us keep our perspective about where we need to be in our relationship with God.

2 Corinthians 7:1

> *Let us work toward complete purity because we fear God.*

A healthy fear of God motivates us to strive for holiness.

Deuteronomy 31:7-8

> *Be strong and courageous! . . . Do not be afraid or discouraged, for the LORD is the one who goes before you.*

Fear can be good if it teaches us about courage. Joshua couldn't have truly understood courage if he hadn't experienced fear. Fear gave him courageous character and taught him to rely on and trust in God.

WHEN IS FEAR NOT GOOD?

Genesis 26:7

> *He was afraid to admit that she was his wife.*

Joshua 17:16

> *The Canaanites . . . have iron chariots—they are too strong for us.*

Fear is not good if it keeps us from doing the things we ought to do. We are not meant to live in fear.

PROMISE FROM GOD:

Isaiah 41:10

> *Don't be afraid, for I am with you. Do not be dismayed, for I am your God. I will strengthen you. I will help you. I will uphold you with my victorious right hand.*

Forgiveness

DO I HAVE TO FORGIVE OTHERS WHO HURT ME?

Matthew 6:14-15

> *If you forgive those who sin against you, your heavenly Father will forgive you. But if you refuse to forgive others, your Father will not forgive your sins.*

Mark 11:25

> *When you are praying, first forgive anyone you are holding a grudge against, so that your Father in heaven will forgive your sins, too.*

We will receive God's forgiveness only when we forgive others who have wronged us.

Matthew 18:21-22

> *Peter came to him and asked, "Lord, how often should I forgive someone who sins against me? Seven times?" "No!" Jesus replied, "seventy times seven!"*

Just as God forgives us without limit, we should forgive others without counting how many times.

Luke 17.3

> *If another believer sins, rebuke him; then if he repents, forgive him.*

Forgiveness doesn't have to be cheap. Love can be tough.

Luke 23.34

> *Jesus said, "Father, forgive these people, because they don't know what they are doing."*

Jesus forgave those who mocked him and killed him.

Colossians 3.13

> *You must make allowance for each other's faults and forgive the person who offends you. Remember, the Lord forgave you, so you must forgive others.*

1 Peter 3.8

> *Don't repay evil for evil. Don't retaliate when people say unkind things about you. Instead, pay them back with a blessing. That is what God wants you to do, and he will bless you for it.*

God wants us to respond to others' sins by blessing them.

IS THERE A LIMIT TO HOW MUCH GOD WILL FORGIVE ME?

Isaiah 1.18

> *"Come now, let us argue this out," says the LORD. "No matter how deep the stain of your sins, I can remove it. I can make you as clean as freshly fallen snow. Even if you are stained as red as crimson, I can make you as white as wool."*

Joel 2:32
> *Anyone who calls on the name of the LORD will be saved.*

No matter how sinful and disobedient we have been, we can receive God's forgiveness by turning to him in repentance.

Psalm 86:5
> *O Lord, you are so good, so ready to forgive, so full of unfailing love for all who ask your aid.*

Psalm 103:3
> *He forgives all my sins and heals all my diseases.*

Ezekiel 18:22
> *All their past sins will be forgotten, and they will live because of the righteous things they have done.*

God is ready to forgive us.

Matthew 18:23-27
> *The Kingdom of Heaven can be compared to a king who decided to bring his accounts up to date. . . . One of his debtors was brought in who owed him millions of dollars. He couldn't pay. . . . Then the king was filled with pity for him, and he released him and forgave his debt.*

God is merciful toward us even though our debt is so great.

Luke 24:47
> *With my authority, take this message of repentance to all the nations, beginning in Jerusalem: "There is forgiveness of sins for all who turn to me."*

Ephesians 1:7
> *He is so rich in kindness that he purchased our freedom through the blood of his Son, and our sins are forgiven.*

Colossians 1:14
> *God has purchased our freedom with his blood and has forgiven all our sins.*

God is willing to forgive every sin because Christ has already paid the penalty for all sin by his death.

Mark 3:29
> *Anyone who blasphemes against the Holy Spirit will never be forgiven. It is an eternal sin.*

Those who harden themselves against God's Spirit and reject him utterly will never experience his forgiveness.

PROMISE FROM GOD:
1 John 1:9
> *If we confess our sins to him, he is faithful and just to forgive us and to cleanse us from every wrong.*

Friendship

WHAT IS THE MARK OF TRUE FRIENDSHIP?

Proverbs 17:17

A friend is always loyal, and a brother is born to help in time of need.

1 Samuel 18:3

Jonathan made a special vow to be David's friend.

Some friendships are fleeting, and some are lasting. True friendships are glued together with bonds of loyalty and commitment. They remain intact despite changing external circumstances.

WHAT GETS IN THE WAY OF FRIENDSHIPS?

1 Samuel 18:9-11

From that time on Saul kept a jealous eye on David. . . . Saul, who had a spear in his hand, suddenly hurled it at David.

Jealousy is the great dividing force of friendships. Envy over what a friend has can quickly turn to anger and bitterness, causing you to separate yourself from the one you truly cared for.

Psalm 41:9

Even my best friend, the one I trusted completely . . . has turned against me.

When respect or reverence is seriously damaged, even the closest friendship is at risk.

2 Samuel 13:11

> As she was feeding him, he grabbed her and demanded, "Come to bed with me."

Friendships are destroyed when boundaries are violated.

Genesis 50:17, 21

> "We . . . beg you to forgive us." . . . "No, don't be afraid. Indeed, I myself will take care of you."

Forgiveness restores broken relationships.

What do I do when I'm having trouble making friends?

Job 19:19

> My close friends abhor me. Those I loved have turned against me.

John 5:7

> I have no one to help me into the pool.

We all go through times when it seems that our friends have deserted us.

John 15:15

> I no longer call you servants. . . . Now you are my friends.

Hebrews 13:5

> I will never fail you. I will never forsake you.

The first thing we must do is remember that God is our constant friend and will never leave us.

Ephesians 4:32

> *Instead, be kind to each other, tenderhearted, forgiving one another, just as God through Christ has forgiven you.*

Acts of kindness and generosity attract others to you.

PROMISE FROM GOD:

Matthew 18:20

> *Where two or three gather together because they are mine, I am there among them.*

Fun

CAN I BE A CHRISTIAN AND STILL HAVE FUN?

Nehemiah 8:10

> *Go and celebrate with a feast . . . and share gifts of food with people who have nothing prepared. This is a sacred day. . . . Don't be . . . sad, for the joy of the LORD is your strength!*

Matthew 25:21

> *You have been faithful in handling this small amount. . . . Let's celebrate together!*

Proverbs 13:9

> *The life of the godly is full of light and joy, but the sinner's light is snuffed out.*

1 Timothy 3:2

> *He must enjoy having guests in his home.*

Joy, fun, and celebration, as God intended, are important parts of Christian faith because these things lift our spirits and help us to see the beauty and meaning in life.

WHAT KINDS OF THINGS ARE INAPPROPRIATE WHEN HAVING FUN?

1 Peter 4:3

> *You have had enough in the past of the evil things that godless people enjoy . . . their feasting and drunkenness and wild parties.*

Fun is wrong when it is self-centered or indulgent, when it involves sinful acts, or when it has conditions that can tempt you into sin.

God's Will

DOES GOD HAVE A PLAN FOR MY LIFE?

Psalm 139:3

> *You chart the path ahead of me and tell me where to stop and rest. Every moment you know where I am.*

God cares about what we do. He cares about the details of our life because they are a barometer of the condition of our heart.

Psalm 138:8

The LORD will work out his plans for my life.

God's plans for us are always for good. Unknown plans can be frightening, but when the plans belong to God, we can rest assured that we can expect something marvelous.

Psalm 32:8

The LORD says, "I will guide you along the best pathway for your life. I will advise you and watch over you."

God wants to help us follow the path that will be most pleasing to *him*, not the path that may be most pleasing to us.

WHAT ARE SOME THINGS I SHOULD DO TO DISCOVER GOD'S WILL FOR MY LIFE?

Proverbs 2:3-5

Cry out for insight and understanding. Search for them as you would for lost money or hidden treasure. Then you will understand what it means to fear the LORD.

Actively look for God's will for you.

Isaiah 2:3

Come, let us go up to the mountain of the LORD, to the Temple of the God of Israel. There he will teach us his ways, so that we may obey him.

Let God teach you from his Word.

Hosea 6:3

> *Oh, that we might know the LORD! Let us press on to know him! Then he will respond to us.*

Give yourself completely to knowing his will. Seek God's will passionately, not casually.

Proverbs 2:6

> *The LORD grants wisdom!*

James 1:5

> *If you want to know what God wants you to do—ask him, and he will gladly tell you. He will not resent your asking.*

1 John 5:14

> *We can be confident that he will listen to us whenever we ask him for anything in line with his will.*

Pray, asking God to reveal his will to you.

Acts 21:14

> *When it was clear that we couldn't persuade him, we gave up and said, "The will of the Lord be done."*

Sometimes God's will for us becomes evident through circumstances that are beyond our control and, thus, in his hands.

WHAT ARE SOME OF THE THINGS THAT WE KNOW ARE GOD'S WILL FOR US?

Amos 5:24

> *I want to see a mighty flood of justice, a river of righteous living that will never run dry.*

God's will is that we seek justice at all times and that we do what is right.

1 Corinthians 14:1

> *Let love be your highest goal.*

God's will is that we love others.

Mark 10:45

> *Even I, the Son of Man, came here not to be served but to serve others.*

God's will is that we serve others, putting them above ourselves.

Exodus 20:1

> *God instructed the people.*

God's will is that we obey his laws for living.

Galatians 5:22

> *When the Holy Spirit controls our lives, he will produce . . . fruit in us.*

God's will is that we live under the power and guidance of the Holy Spirit.

Proverbs 16:3

Commit your work to the LORD, and then your plans will succeed.

God's will is that we do everything as if we were doing it for him.

PROMISE FROM GOD:

Jeremiah 29:11

"I know the plans I have for you," says the LORD. "They are plans for good and not for disaster, to give you a future and a hope."

Gossip

WHY IS GOSSIP SO BAD?

Leviticus 19:16

Do not spread slanderous gossip among your people.

Gossip is specifically forbidden by God.

Proverbs 11:13

A gossip goes around revealing secrets, but those who are trustworthy can keep a confidence.

Gossiping often involves breaking another's trust.

Romans 1:29

> *Their lives became full of every kind of wickedness, sin, greed, hate,*
> *envy, murder, fighting, deception, malicious behavior, and gossip.*

God catalogs gossip with greed, hate, envy, and murder.

1 Timothy 5:13

> *They are likely to become lazy and spend their time gossiping*
> *. . . getting into other people's business and saying things they*
> *shouldn't.*

Gossiping often grows out of laziness. When we have nothing
better to do than sit around talking about other people, we may
wind up saying things we will later regret.

Matthew 7:1

> *Stop judging others, and you will not be judged.*

Gossiping puts us in the place of judging others. In a court of
law, rumors and opinions are not allowed because they might
unjustly sway the opinion of the jury. So it is when we turn our
living rooms into courtrooms where we sit as judge and allow
rumor and opinion to color and often damage the reputation of
others who have no chance to defend themselves.

Proverbs 18:8

> *What dainty morsels rumors are—but they sink deep into one's*
> *heart.*

Gossip hurts others. It also destroys your credibility if the gossip
proves false.

How do I stop gossip?

Proverbs 26.20

> *Fire goes out for lack of fuel, and quarrels disappear when gossip stops.*

Stop the chain of gossip with you! When you hear gossip, you can do something about it. You can decide not to spread it any further. Stop the fires of gossip from spreading beyond you.

Deuteronomy 13.14

> *You must examine the facts carefully.*

If you are not sure something is gossip, you must look carefully into the matter without assuming that what you have been told is true. Go to the source and get the facts straight.

Matthew 7.12

> *Do for others what you would like them to do for you.*

The Golden Rule can also be applied to our speech: Talk about others in the same way you would like them to talk about you.

Ephesians 4.29

> *Let everything you say be good and helpful, so that your words will be an encouragement to those who hear them.*

If we focus on what is good and helpful, gossip will find no foothold in our heart.

Colossians 3.17

> *Whatever you do or say, let it be as a representative of the Lord Jesus.*

If you think you may be about to gossip, ask yourself, *Does the person I'm talking to need to know this? Is it true, accurate, and helpful?*

PROMISE FROM GOD:

1 Peter 3:10

> *The Scriptures say, "If you want a happy life and good days, keep your tongue from speaking evil, and keep your lips from telling lies."*

Habits

WHAT ARE SOME OF THE BAD HABITS THE BIBLE TALKS ABOUT?

1 John 3:8

> *When people keep on sinning, it shows they belong to the Devil.*

Sin is a habit none of us can beat completely, but a pattern of sinful living shows that we may not be serious about following God.

Exodus 8:28, 32

> *"All right, go ahead," Pharaoh replied. "I will let you go. . . ." But Pharaoh hardened his heart again and refused to let the people go.*

Pharaoh developed a bad habit of lying and wanting his own way. We can easily slip into these same habits, but that is disastrous.

Numbers 11:1

The people soon began to complain . . . about their hardships.

The Israelites developed a bad habit of complaining. Chronic complaining can quickly turn into bitterness.

1 Timothy 5:13

They are likely to become lazy and spend their time gossiping.

Too much time and too little to do can be fertile ground for bad habits. Idleness makes it easy to develop the bad habit of gossip.

HOW DO WE DEAL WITH BAD HABITS?

Romans 7:15

I don't understand myself at all, for I really want to do what is right, but I don't do it. Instead, I do the very thing I hate.

Have you ever felt this way? Paul reveals to us one of the best ways to deal with bad habits—recognize them for what they are and confess them honestly. Paul knew that he could not kick the habit of sin overnight. But he knew that, with God's help, he could make progress every day. In the same way, we may have to give up a habit in phases, one day at a time.

1 John 2:15

Stop loving this evil world and all that it offers you.

Sin often appears lovely and attractive. In the same way, bad habits often feel good even though we know they are ultimately bad for us. Breaking a bad habit can be hard because we are losing something we like. There may be a grieving process, but pain over losing a bad habit brings a deeper joy because we are doing what is pleasing to God.

Colossians 3:2
> *Let heaven fill your thoughts.*

We must replace a bad habit with something good.

HOW DO WE DEVELOP GOOD HABITS?

Hebrews 10:25
> *Let us not neglect our meeting together, as some people do.*

Meeting together as believers is a good habit because it provides necessary fellowship with other believers, it develops the habit of group Bible study, it keeps us busy when we might otherwise be slipping into bad habits, and it offers an accountability group.

Genesis 26:21-22
> *Isaac's men then dug another well, but again there was a fight over it. . . . Abandoning that one, he dug another well, and the local people finally left him alone.*

Isaac pursued a habit of peace.

Psalm 28:7
> *The LORD is my strength, my shield from every danger. I trust in him with all my heart. . . . I burst out in songs of thanksgiving.*

As a young boy, David developed the habit of talking to God, singing songs about him, and writing psalms. This helped him to trust in and follow God all his life.

PROMISE FROM GOD:

Romans 8:5

> Those who are dominated by the sinful nature think about sinful things, but those who are controlled by the Holy Spirit think about things that please the Spirit.

Happiness

HOW CAN I BRING HAPPINESS TO GOD?

Deuteronomy 30:10

> The LORD your God will delight in you if you obey his voice and keep the commands and laws written in this Book of the Law, and if you turn to the LORD your God with all your heart and soul.

Proverbs 11:1

> The LORD . . . delights in honesty.

Proverbs 11:20

> The LORD . . . delights in those who have integrity.

Proverbs 15:8

> The LORD . . . delights in the prayers of the upright.

Proverbs 15:26

> The LORD . . . delights in pure words.

Can we finite, sinful human beings truly bring joy and delight to the Lord, the Creator of the universe? Yes, and it is simple though not easy: we bring delight to God by honoring him, obeying him, responding to his love, seeking his forgiveness, and walking daily with him.

HOW DOES GOD EXPRESS HIS HAPPINESS WITH ME?

Zephaniah 3:17

> *The LORD your God has arrived to live among you. He is a mighty savior. He will rejoice over you with great gladness. With his love, he will calm all your fears. He will exult over you by singing a happy song.*

Psalm 18:19

> *He led me to a place of safety; he rescued me because he delights in me.*

Psalm 149:4

> *The LORD delights in his people; he crowns the humble with salvation.*

The Lord delights in saving us from our sins, guiding us in his ways, and daily taking care of us.

WHAT IS THE SOURCE OF TRUE HAPPINESS?

Psalm 40:16

> *May all who search for you be filled with joy and gladness. May those who love your salvation repeatedly shout, "The LORD is great!"*

Psalm 68:3

> *Let the godly rejoice. Let them be glad in God's presence. Let them be filled with joy.*

Psalm 86:4

> *Give me happiness, O Lord, for my life depends on you.*

Psalm 146:5

> *Happy are those who have the God of Israel as their helper, whose hope is in the LORD their God.*

The Lord himself is the wellspring of true happiness. The more we love him, know him, walk with him, and become like him, the greater our happiness.

HOW CAN I BRING HAPPINESS TO OTHERS?

Romans 12:10

> *Love each other with genuine affection, and take delight in honoring each other.*

2 Corinthians 7:13

> *In addition to our own encouragement, we were especially delighted to see how happy Titus was at the way you welcomed him and set his mind at ease.*

Ecclesiastes 9:9

> *Live happily with the woman you love through all the meaningless days of life that God has given you in this world. The wife God gives you is your reward for all your earthly toil.*

As God is the wellspring of true happiness, so we are the conduits of that happiness to others.

PROMISE FROM GOD:

Proverbs 11:23

> *The godly can look forward to happiness, while the wicked can expect only wrath.*

Heaven

IS THERE REALLY A HEAVEN?

Genesis 14:22

> *Abram replied, "I have solemnly promised the LORD, God Most High, Creator of heaven and earth."*

John 14:2

> *There are many rooms in my Father's home, and I am going to prepare a place for you. If this were not so, I would tell you plainly.*

2 Corinthians 5:1

> *For we know that when this earthly tent we live in is taken down—when we die and leave these bodies—we will have a home in heaven.*

Not only is there a heaven, but Jesus is preparing it for our arrival.

WHAT IS HEAVEN LIKE?

Isaiah 65:17

> *Look! I am creating new heavens and a new earth—so wonderful that no one will even think about the old ones anymore.*

Philippians 3:21

> *He will take these weak mortal bodies of ours and change them into glorious bodies like his own.*

144

James 1:17

> *Whatever is good and perfect comes to us from God above, who created all heaven's lights.*

Revelation 21:3-4

> *I heard a loud shout from the throne, saying, "Look, the home of God is now among his people! He will live with them, and they will be his people. God himself will be with them. He will remove all of their sorrows, and there will be no more death or sorrow or crying or pain. For the old world and its evils are gone forever."*

Revelation 22:5

> *There will be no night there—no need for lamps or sun—for the Lord God will shine on them. And they will reign forever and ever.*

In heaven we will live forever with God. There will be no sadness, no pain, no evil, no death. Everything will be perfect and glorious. God will give us each a new body, and we will be able to talk face-to-face with the Lord himself.

WHO WILL GET INTO HEAVEN?

Matthew 5:3

> *God blesses those who realize their need for him, for the Kingdom of Heaven is given to them.*

Matthew 19:14

> *Jesus said, "Let the children come to me. Don't stop them! For the Kingdom of Heaven belongs to such as these."*

John 3:16

> *God so loved the world that he gave his only Son, so that*
> *everyone who believes in him will not perish but have eternal*
> *life.*

Those who accept Jesus Christ as Savior and recognize that only he can forgive their sins will gain entrance into heaven. This occurs only with a humble and repentant attitude.

DOES THE BIBLE REALLY CLAIM THAT THERE IS ONLY ONE WAY TO HEAVEN?

John 14:6

> *Jesus told him, "I am the way, the truth, and the life. No one*
> *can come to the Father except through me."*

Jesus is the only way to heaven. We may want to buy our way in, work our way in, think our way in. But the Bible is clear—Jesus Christ provides the only way in.

PROMISE FROM GOD:

1 Corinthians 2:9

> *No eye has seen, no ear has heard, and no mind has imagined*
> *what God has prepared for those who love him.*

Hell

IS THERE REALLY A PLACE CALLED HELL?

Matthew 7:13

> *You can enter God's Kingdom only through the narrow gate.*
> *The highway to hell is broad, and its gate is wide for the many*
> *who choose the easy way.*

Matthew 13:49-50

> *That is the way it will be at the end of the world. The angels*
> *will come and separate the wicked people from the godly,*
> *throwing the wicked into the fire.*

2 Peter 2:4

> *God did not spare even the angels when they sinned; he threw*
> *them into hell.*

Revelation 20:10

> *The Devil . . . was thrown into the lake of fire that burns with*
> *sulfur. . . . There they will be tormented day and night forever*
> *and ever.*

Although we don't know where hell is, it definitely exists.

WHAT IS HELL LIKE?

2 Peter 2:4

> *God did not spare even the angels when they sinned; he threw*
> *them into hell, in gloomy caves and darkness.*

Revelation 19:20

> *Both the beast and his false prophet were thrown alive into the lake of fire that burns with sulfur.*

Jude 1:7

> *Those cities [Sodom and Gomorrah] were destroyed by fire and are a warning of the eternal fire that will punish all who are evil.*

Luke 16:22-24

> *The rich man also died and was buried, and his soul went to the place of the dead. There, in torment, he saw Lazarus in the far distance with Abraham. The rich man shouted, "Father Abraham, have some pity! Send Lazarus over here to dip the tip of his finger in water and cool my tongue, because I am in anguish in these flames."*

Our imagination cannot comprehend how horrible hell is. Here on earth we tend to think in time spans that have a beginning and an end. There will be no end to hell.

WHO WILL BE SENT TO HELL?

Jude 1:15

> *He will bring the people of the world to judgment. He will convict the ungodly of all the evil things they have done in rebellion and of all the insults that godless sinners have spoken against him.*

Revelation 20:15

> *Anyone whose name was not found recorded in the Book of Life was thrown into the lake of fire.*

All who have not received eternal life through faith in Christ will spend eternity in hell.

How can I be assured that I am not going to hell?

John 3:16

> God so loved the world that he gave his only Son, so that everyone who believes in him will not perish but have eternal life.

John 14:6

> Jesus told him, "I am the way, the truth, and the life. No one can come to the Father except through me."

1 John 4:17

> As we live in God, our love grows more perfect. So we will not be afraid on the day of judgment, but we can face him with confidence because we are like Christ here in this world.

Romans 10:9

> If you confess with your mouth that Jesus is Lord and believe in your heart that God raised him from the dead, you will be saved.

There is only one way to be certain that you are included in the Book of Life. You must confess your sin and believe in Jesus Christ as your personal Savior. By taking this step, you secure your place in heaven, and you don't have to fear hell.

Homosexuality

IS HOMOSEXUALITY WRONG?

Leviticus 18.22

Do not practice homosexuality; it is a detestable sin.

The Bible is clear about the practice of homosexuality. God views it as a sin.

ARE PEOPLE BORN HOMOSEXUAL?

Leviticus 20.13

The penalty for homosexual acts is death to both parties. They have committed a detestable act and are guilty of a capital offense.

It would be contrary to God's character for him to create a person to be homosexual when his laws call for death because of it.

IF PEOPLE AREN'T BORN HOMOSEXUAL, THEN WHERE DO THOSE FEELINGS COME FROM?

Romans 1.21-24

They knew God, but they wouldn't worship him as God or even give him thanks. And they began to think up foolish ideas of what God was like. The result was that their minds became dark and confused. . . . So God let them go ahead and do whatever shameful things their hearts desired. As a result, they did vile and degrading things with each other's bodies.

Sin causes unnatural feelings within us. Only by staying close to God on a daily basis can we overcome the temptations that constantly face us.

HOW CAN PEOPLE OVERCOME THEIR HOMOSEXUAL FEELINGS?

1 Corinthians 10:13

Remember that the temptations that come into your life are no different from what others experience. And God is faithful. He will keep the temptation from becoming so strong that you can't stand up against it. When you are tempted, he will show you a way out so that you will not give in to it.

James 1:12

God blesses the people who patiently endure testing. Afterward they will receive the crown of life that God has promised to those who love him.

James 4:17

Remember, it is sin to know what you ought to do and then not do it.

People can overcome homosexual feelings in the same way that people can overcome heterosexual temptations—by looking to God for help, resolving to stand firm, and avoiding tempting situations.

CAN GOD FORGIVE HOMOSEXUAL BEHAVIOR?

Hebrews 8:12

I will forgive their wrongdoings, and I will never again remember their sins.

1 John 1:9

> *If we confess our sins to him, he is faithful and just to forgive us and to cleanse us from every wrong.*

Hebrews 4:16

> *So let us come boldly to the throne of our gracious God. There we will receive his mercy, and we will find grace to help us when we need it.*

When we confess our sin to God, he not only forgives us but also gives us new life. He will change our heart and make us new people, free from the imprisonment of our past sins.

PROMISE FROM GOD:

1 Corinthians 6:9-10

> *Don't you know that those who do wrong will have no share in the Kingdom of God? Don't fool yourselves. Those who indulge in sexual sin, who are idol worshipers, adulterers, male prostitutes, homosexuals . . . none of these will have a share in the Kingdom of God.*

Honesty

WHY IS IT SO IMPORTANT TO BE HONEST?

Psalm 24:3-4

> *Who may climb the mountain of the LORD? Who may stand in his holy place? Only those whose hands and hearts are pure, who do not worship idols and never tell lies.*

Honesty is necessary for us to live in God's presence.

Proverbs 16:11
> *The LORD demands fairness in every business deal; he sets the standard.*

God expects us to be honest.

Proverbs 12:5
> *The plans of the godly are just.*

Matthew 12:33
> *A tree is identified by its fruit.*

Luke 16:10
> *If you cheat even a little, you won't be honest with greater responsibilities.*

People's honesty or dishonesty reveals just what kind of people they are.

1 Timothy 1:19
> *Always keep your conscience clear. For some people have deliberately violated their consciences; as a result, their faith has been shipwrecked.*

Honesty brings a clear conscience.

Deuteronomy 25:13-15
> *You must use accurate scales when you weigh out merchandise, and you must use full and honest measures . . . so that you will enjoy a long life.*

God blesses us when we are concerned not about how much we get but about being honest in getting it.

Proverbs 11:3
> *Good people are guided by their honesty; treacherous people are destroyed by their dishonesty.*

Dishonesty and deception are forms of bondage because we are always trying to hide our real motives. There is freedom in honesty because it allows for forgiveness, vulnerability, positive change, and healing.

Romans 12:3
> *Be honest in your estimate of yourselves.*

Honestly evaluating our walk with the Lord is the only way to keep growing in faith.

PROMISE FROM GOD:

Psalm 37:37
> *Look at those who are honest and good, for a wonderful future lies before those who love peace.*

Hope

WHERE DOES HOPE COME FROM?

Psalm 39:7

> *Lord, where do I put my hope? My only hope is in you.*

Psalm 71:5

> *O Lord, you alone are my hope. I've trusted you, O LORD, from childhood.*

The Lord himself is the source of hope because he determines our future.

WHY SHOULD I TRUST GOD AS MY HOPE?

Hebrews 6:18-19

> *God has given us both his promise and his oath. These two things are unchangeable because it is impossible for God to lie. Therefore, we who have fled to him for refuge can take new courage, for we can hold on to his promise with confidence. This confidence is like a strong and trustworthy anchor for our souls. It leads us through the curtain of heaven into God's inner sanctuary.*

Hebrews 10:23

> *Without wavering, let us hold tightly to the hope we say we have, for God can be trusted to keep his promise.*

1 Peter 1:21

> *Through Christ you have come to trust in God. And because God raised Christ from the dead and gave him great glory, your faith and hope can be placed confidently in God.*

God cannot lie, because he *is* truth. God, therefore, cannot break his promises. His word stands forever. God must be trusted as our hope because he alone conquered death by raising Christ from the dead.

WHERE CAN I GO DAILY TO REINFORCE MY HOPE?

Romans 15:4

> *Such things were written in the Scriptures long ago to teach us. They give us hope and encouragement as we wait patiently for God's promises.*

Psalm 119:43, 74, 81, 114, 147

> *Do not snatch your word of truth from me, for my only hope is in your laws. . . . May all who fear you find in me a cause for joy, for I have put my hope in your word. . . . I faint with longing for your salvation; but I have put my hope in your word. . . . You are my refuge and my shield; your word is my only source of hope. . . . I rise early, before the sun is up; I cry out for help and put my hope in your words.*

Each day we can visit God's word and have our hope renewed and reinforced. His word never fails or wavers.

How does hope help me live better today?

Philippians 3.13-14

> *No, dear brothers and sisters, I am still not all I should be, but I am focusing all my energies on this one thing: Forgetting the past and looking forward to what lies ahead, I strain to reach the end of the race and receive the prize for which God, through Christ Jesus, is calling us up to heaven.*

Hope helps us focus on our future, especially our eternal future, and gives us energy to press on in our daily tasks.

1 John 3.3

> *All who believe this will keep themselves pure, just as Christ is pure.*

Hope helps us keep our life pure before God.

How is hope related to God's plan for me?

Jeremiah 29.11

> *"I know the plans I have for you," says the LORD. "They are plans for good and not for disaster, to give you a future and a hope."*

Romans 12.12

> *Be glad for all God is planning for you. Be patient in trouble, and always be prayerful.*

Our future will involve what God has planned for us. We know that his plans are to bless us, so we can look forward to our future with joyful hope and anticipation.

PROMISE FROM GOD:
Psalm 71:5

O Lord, you alone are my hope.

Humility

WHAT IS TRUE HUMILITY?
Zephaniah 3:12

Those who are left will be the lowly and the humble, for it is they who trust in the name of the LORD.

Humility is not thinking too highly of yourself.

Matthew 18:4

Anyone who becomes as humble as this little child is the greatest in the Kingdom of Heaven.

Humility is childlikeness.

Titus 3:2

They must not speak evil of anyone, and they must avoid quarreling. Instead, they should be gentle and show true humility to everyone.

Humility is gentleness.

Psalm 51:3-4

> *I recognize my shameful deeds—they haunt me day and night. Against you, and you alone, have I sinned; I have done what is evil in your sight. You will be proved right in what you say, and your judgment against me is just.*

Humility is willingness to confess sin.

Proverbs 12:23

> *Wise people don't make a show of their knowledge, but fools broadcast their folly.*

Humility is not having to prove yourself.

Proverbs 13:10

> *Pride leads to arguments; those who take advice are wise.*

Humility allows us to take advice.

How is God's Son humble?

Zechariah 9:9

> *Rejoice greatly, O people of Zion! Shout in triumph, O people of Jerusalem! Look, your king is coming to you. He is righteous and victorious, yet he is humble, riding on a donkey—even on a donkey's colt.*

Jesus was King of kings, yet in his royal procession he rode on a donkey.

Philippians 2:5-11

> *Your attitude should be the same that Christ Jesus had. Though he was God, he did not demand and cling to his rights as God. He made himself nothing; he took the humble position of a slave and appeared in human form. And in human form he obediently humbled himself even further by dying a criminal's death on a cross. Because of this, God raised him up to the heights of heaven and gave him a name that is above every other name, so that at the name of Jesus every knee will bow, in heaven and on earth and under the earth, and every tongue will confess that Jesus Christ is Lord, to the glory of God the Father.*

Jesus is God, yet he made himself nothing and suffered death on the cross for us.

Hebrews 2:9

> *What we do see is Jesus, who "for a little while was made lower than the angels" and now is "crowned with glory and honor" because he suffered death for us. Yes, by God's grace, Jesus tasted death for everyone in all the world.*

Jesus had all the glory and honor, but for our sake he died so that we could be saved and have eternal life with him.

Matthew 11:29

> *Take my yoke upon you. Let me teach you, because I am humble and gentle, and you will find rest for your souls.*

Jesus' way of dealing with people and teaching them demonstrates humility.

HOW DO I BECOME HUMBLE?

Deuteronomy 8:2-3

> Remember how the LORD your God led you through the
> wilderness for forty years, humbling you and testing you to prove
> your character, and to find out whether or not you would really
> obey his commands. Yes, he humbled you by letting you go
> hungry and then feeding you with manna. . . . He did it to
> teach you that people need more than bread for their life.

Humility comes when we recognize that we need God and then
watch him meet our needs!

1 Peter 3:8

> All of you should be of one mind, full of sympathy toward each
> other, loving one another with tender hearts and humble minds.

Humility comes from developing sympathetic and tender hearts
toward others.

Philippians 2:3

> Don't be selfish; don't live to make a good impression on others.
> Be humble, thinking of others as better than yourself.

Humility means thinking of others as better than yourself.

1 Peter 5:5

> You younger men, accept the authority of the elders. And all of
> you, serve each other in humility, for "God sets himself against
> the proud, but he shows favor to the humble."

Humility means accepting the authority of those who are over us.

•

HOW DOES GOD RESPOND TO THE HUMBLE?

Psalm 25:9

He leads the humble in what is right, teaching them his way.

God leads and teaches the humble.

Psalm 149:4

The LORD delights in his people; he crowns the humble with salvation.

The Lord takes delight in the humble and offers them salvation.

1 Peter 5:6

Humble yourselves under the mighty power of God, and in his good time he will honor you.

The Lord honors the humble.

Daniel 10:12

Since the first day you began to pray for understanding and to humble yourself before your God, your request has been heard in heaven. I have come in answer to your prayer.

God acknowledges the prayers of the humble.

Psalm 69:32

The humble will see their God at work and be glad. Let all who seek God's help live in joy.

Humility opens our eyes to see God at work in our life.

WHAT IS THE VALUE OF A HUMBLE SPIRIT?

2 Samuel 22:28

> *You rescue those who are humble, but your eyes are on the proud to humiliate them.*

God rescues the humble.

Proverbs 15:33

> *Fear of the LORD teaches a person to be wise; humility precedes honor.*

Matthew 23:12

> *Those who exalt themselves will be humbled, and those who humble themselves will be exalted.*

God honors and exalts the humble.

Deuteronomy 8:16

> *He fed you with manna in the wilderness, a food unknown to your ancestors. He did this to humble you and test you for your own good.*

Humility strengthens our character—it is for our own good.

Proverbs 11:2

> *Pride leads to disgrace, but with humility comes wisdom.*

Humility leads to wisdom.

HOW CAN HUMILITY HELP ME DEAL WITH SIN?

James 4:6-10

> *He gives us more and more strength to stand against such evil desires. As the Scriptures say, "God sets himself against the proud, but he shows favor to the humble." So humble yourselves before God. Resist the Devil, and he will flee from you. Draw close to God, and God will draw close to you. Wash your hands, you sinners; purify your hearts, you hypocrites. Let there be tears for the wrong things you have done. . . . When you bow down before the Lord and admit your dependence on him, he will lift you up and give you honor.*

Humility is essential to recognizing the sin in our life, admitting that we need God, and seeking his forgiveness. A proud person cannot do this.

PROMISE FROM GOD:

Matthew 23:12

> *Those who exalt themselves will be humbled, and those who humble themselves will be exalted.*

Inferiority

WHAT CAN I DO TO MAKE MY LIFE SEEM MORE WORTHWHILE?

Acts 20:24

> *My life is worth nothing unless I use it for doing the work assigned me by the Lord Jesus—the work of telling others the Good News about God's wonderful kindness and love.*

Paul found that the secret to a worthwhile life was to fulfill God's purpose. When we do the things that please God, we will find meaning and purpose in our life.

HOW CAN I DEAL WITH FEELINGS OF INFERIORITY?

Genesis 1:26

> God said, "Let us make people in our image, to be like ourselves. They will be masters over all life—the fish in the sea, the birds in the sky, and all the livestock, wild animals, and small animals."

Everyone faces times when they are not feeling confident, when they feel insignificant. When these times arise, remember that God created you in his image and you have many of the characteristics of God himself. He created you with a purpose. Criticizing yourself is criticizing the wonderful way God has made you.

2 Corinthians 5:15

> He died for everyone so that those who receive his new life will no longer live to please themselves. Instead, they will live to please Christ, who died and was raised for them.

God loves us so much that he sent his Son, Jesus, to die for us. He didn't die just for the rich or influential but for everyone, no matter what their station in life. This alone should give us a great sense of self-worth!

PROMISE FROM GOD:

Psalm 139:17

> How precious are your thoughts about me, O God!

Insignificance: *see* **Inferiority**

Jealousy

WHY IS JEALOUSY SO DANGEROUS?

Proverbs 14:30

> *A relaxed attitude lengthens life; jealousy rots it away.*

Jealousy brings decay to our life because it causes us to focus on anger and bitterness.

Genesis 13:7

> *An argument broke out between the herdsmen of Abram and Lot.*

Proverbs 27:4

> *Anger is cruel . . . but who can survive the destructiveness of jealousy?*

Jealousy tears families and friends apart. Jealousy drove Lot's herdsmen to fight with his uncle Abram's herdsmen.

WHAT DOES IT MEAN THAT GOD IS A "JEALOUS GOD"?

Exodus 34:14

> *You must worship no other gods, but only the LORD, for he is a God who is passionate about his relationship with you.*

Deuteronomy 5:9

> I, the LORD your God, am a jealous God who will not share
> your affection with any other god!

Deuteronomy 32:21

> They have roused my jealousy by worshiping non-gods.

Zechariah 1:14

> This is what the LORD Almighty says: My love for Jerusalem
> and Mount Zion is passionate and strong.

When people give their honor, praise, and love to other things,
God is jealous that the honor due him has been squandered
elsewhere.

WHERE DOES JEALOUSY TAKE US? WHAT CAN HAPPEN NEXT?

Proverbs 12:12

> Thieves are jealous of each other's loot, while the godly bear
> their own fruit.

Jealousy easily leads to coveting and to theft. Godliness, on the
other hand, leads to a life filled with the fruit of the Spirit.

Genesis 4:4-5

> The LORD accepted Abel and his offering, but he did not accept
> Cain and his offering. This made Cain very angry.

Galatians 5:22-23

> When the Holy Spirit controls our lives, he will produce this
> kind of fruit in us: love, joy, peace, patience, kindness, goodness,
> faithfulness, gentleness, and self-control.

When we seek the character traits that come from the Holy Spirit, we are spared from petty human jealousies and the hard feelings that come from competition for honor and popularity.

PROMISE FROM GOD:
Mark 11:24-25

> *Listen to me! You can pray for anything, and if you believe, you will have it. But when you are praying, first forgive anyone you are holding a grudge against, so that your Father in heaven will forgive your sins, too.*

Knowledge/Learning

WHY IS LEARNING SO IMPORTANT?
Proverbs 1:4

> *These proverbs will make the simpleminded clever. They will give knowledge and purpose to young people.*

Proper knowledge leads to purpose. Knowledge in Jesus changes our purpose in life. If you are struggling with your purpose in life, spend time studying and getting to know God's Word, and God will reveal his purpose to you.

Proverbs 2:10

> *Wisdom will enter your heart, and knowledge will fill you with joy.*

Using the wisdom God has given us saves us from choosing many wrong paths.

WHAT IS THE MOST IMPORTANT THING TO LEARN?

Proverbs 1:7

> *Fear of the LORD is the beginning of knowledge. Only fools despise wisdom and discipline.*

Proverbs 1:29-31

> *They hated knowledge and chose not to fear the LORD. They rejected my advice and paid no attention when I corrected them. That is why they must eat the bitter fruit of living their own way.*

Learn to fear the Lord. This is not the cowering kind of fear but a fear that shows utmost knowledge and respect of who God is, why he created you, and what he wants you to accomplish with your knowledge.

HOW CAN KNOWLEDGE BE HARMFUL?

Isaiah 47:10-11

> *You felt secure in all your wickedness. "No one sees me," you said. Your "wisdom" and "knowledge" have caused you to turn away from me and claim, "I am self-sufficient and not account-able to anyone!" So disaster will overtake you.*

Knowledge is harmful when it leads us to think we no longer need God. If we think we can rely on our own smarts to make it through this life, we will be deeply disappointed.

PROMISE FROM GOD:

Proverbs 2:3-5

> *Cry out for insight and understanding. Search for them. . . .*
> *Then you will understand what it means to fear the LORD.*

Laziness

WHAT DOES THE BIBLE SAY ABOUT LAZINESS?

Proverbs 10:4

> *Lazy people are soon poor.*

Proverbs 13:4

> *Lazy people want much but get little, but those who work hard*
> *will prosper and be satisfied.*

Proverbs 15:19

> *A lazy person has trouble all through life.*

Romans 12:11

> *Never be lazy in your work, but serve the Lord enthusiastically.*

Laziness brings trouble to a person's life. It is much better to work hard.

IS IT A SIN TO BE LAZY?

Ezekiel 16:49

> *Sodom's sins were pride, laziness, and gluttony.*

2 Thessalonians 3:11

> *We hear that some of you are living idle lives, refusing to work and wasting time meddling in other people's business.*

1 Timothy 5:13

> *They are likely to become lazy and spend their time gossiping from house to house, getting into other people's business and saying things they shouldn't.*

There is a difference between rest and laziness. The Bible clearly says that laziness is sin, while rest is a reward for hard work. Someday we will be asked to give account for how we spent our time here on earth. There is no accounting for laziness, but God has made ample provision for us to get the rest we need along the way.

Loneliness

WHY DOES GOD ALLOW US TO GET LONELY?

Genesis 2:18

> *The LORD God said, "It is not good for the man to be alone. I will make a companion who will help him."*

God did not intend for us to be lonely. Quite the contrary, it was God who recognized Adam's need for companionship. He gave Adam the task of naming the animals so that Adam could recognize his own need for a companion. Then God created woman.

Romans 8.38-39

> *I am convinced that nothing can ever separate us from his love. Death can't, and life can't. The angels can't, and the demons can't. Our fears for today, our worries about tomorrow, and even the powers of hell can't keep God's love away. Whether we are high above the sky or in the deepest ocean, nothing in all creation will ever be able to separate us from the love of God that is revealed in Christ Jesus our Lord.*

God never intended for us to be alone. He has promised us that he will always be there. Nothing can separate us from him. He intended for us to have human, as well as spiritual, relationships.

HOW CAN I AVOID LONELINESS?

Romans 12.5

> *Since we are all one body in Christ, we belong to each other, and each of us needs all the others.*

Hebrews 10.25

> *Let us not neglect our meeting together, as some people do, but encourage and warn each other, especially now that the day of his coming back again is drawing near.*

The best way to avoid loneliness is to get together with other believers. Each of us should be involved in a local church.

HOW CAN GOD HELP ME WITH MY LONELINESS?

Psalm 23.4

> *Even when I walk through the dark valley of death . . . you are close beside me.*

Psalm 139.17

> *How precious are your thoughts about me, O God!*

Isaiah 54.10

> *The mountains may depart and the hills disappear, but even then I will remain loyal to you.*

Recognize that you are not unlovable or deficient just because you are lonely. You have value because God made you, loves you, and promises never to leave you.

Exodus 5.21-22

> *The foremen said to them, "May the LORD judge you for getting us into this terrible situation. . . ." So Moses went back to the LORD and protested . . . "Why did you send me?"*

1 Kings 19.4

> *He sat down under a solitary broom tree and prayed that he might die.*

Don't give up on God when you are lonely. It will cause you to feel sorry for yourself, become discouraged, and fall prey to temptation.

1 Kings 19.10

> *I alone am left, and now they are trying to kill me, too.*

Matthew 11:2-3

> *John the Baptist, who was now in prison . . . sent his disciples to ask Jesus, "Are you really the Messiah we've been waiting for, or should we keep looking for someone else?"*

1 Peter 4:19

> *If you are suffering according to God's will, keep on doing what is right, and trust yourself to the God who made you, for he will never fail you.*

Sometimes we feel alone in our stand for Christ. We can take comfort in knowing that there are others who are equally committed and that God rewards our bold commitment.

Isaiah 41:10

> *Don't be afraid, for I am with you. Do not be dismayed, for I am your God. I will strengthen you. I will help you. I will uphold you with my victorious right hand.*

John 14:1

> *Don't be troubled. You trust God, now trust in me.*

Loneliness can cause us to be afraid, but God calms our fears.

PROMISE FROM GOD:

Psalm 23:4

> *Even when I walk through the dark valley of death . . . you are close beside me.*

Love

MUST I LOVE OTHER PEOPLE? WHAT IF I DON'T WANT TO?

John 13:34-35

> I am giving you a new commandment: Love each other. Just as I have loved you, you should love each other. Your love for one another will prove to the world that you are my disciples.

1 John 2:9

> If anyone says, "I am living in the light" but hates a Christian brother or sister, that person is still living in darkness.

1 Peter 4:8

> Love covers a multitude of sins.

1 John 4:12

> If we love each other, God lives in us, and his love has been brought to full expression through us.

Being a Christian comes with certain expectations. One of them is that we will love others. Our Christian conduct is proof of whether we love each other, and loving each other is proof that we belong to Christ.

WHAT ARE SOME SPECIAL THINGS THAT COME FROM A LOVING RELATIONSHIP?

Proverbs 10:12

> Love covers all offenses.

1 Corinthians 13:4-7

> *Love is patient and kind. Love is not jealous or boastful or*
> *proud or rude. Love does not demand its own way. Love is not*
> *irritable, and it keeps no record of when it has been wronged.*
> *It is never glad about injustice but rejoices whenever the truth*
> *wins out. Love never gives up, never loses faith, is always*
> *hopeful, and endures through every circumstance.*

The gifts that come from love are many, including forgiveness,
patience, kindness, love for truth, love for justice, love for the
best in a person, loyalty at any cost, and belief in a person no
matter what. Love does not allow for jealousy, envy, pride, a
haughty spirit, selfishness, rudeness, a demand for one's own
way, irritability, or grudges.

DOES GOD REALLY LOVE ME? HOW CAN I KNOW?

John 3:16

> *God so loved the world that he gave his only Son, so that*
> *everyone who believes in him will not perish but have eternal*
> *life.*

1 John 4:9-10

> *God showed how much he loved us by sending his only Son into*
> *the world so that we might have eternal life through him. This*
> *is real love.*

We can have absolute certainty that God loves us, because he
sent his Son to suffer in our place and give us eternal life.

Romans 5:5

> *[God] has given us the Holy Spirit to fill our hearts with his love.*

The Holy Spirit's presence in our heart shows us God's love for us.

HOW SHOULD WE SHOW OUR LOVE TO GOD?
Matthew 10:42

If you give even a cup of cold water to one of the least of my followers, you will surely be rewarded.

By showing our love to needy people whom God loves

John 14:21

Those who obey my commandments are the ones who love me.

By obeying him

John 21:15-17

Do you love me? . . . Feed my lambs. . . . Take care of my sheep. . . . Feed my sheep.

Hebrews 6:10

[God] will not forget . . . how you have shown your love to him by caring for other Christians.

By guiding and helping Jesus' followers

Psalm 122:1

I was glad when they said to me, "Let us go to the house of the LORD."

By worshiping him and praising him for his love for us

PROMISE FROM GOD:

Romans 8:39

> *Whether we are high above the sky or in the deepest ocean, nothing in all creation will ever be able to separate us from the love of God that is revealed in Christ Jesus our Lord.*

Lust

IF LUST DOES NOT INVOLVE ACTUAL PHYSICAL BEHAVIOR, WHY IS IT WRONG?

Luke 11:34

> *Your eye is a lamp for your body. A pure eye lets sunshine into your soul. But an evil eye shuts out the light and plunges you into darkness.*

When lust is allowed to take up residence in our mind, it tends to consume our thoughts, and the light of God is pushed aside.

1 Kings 11:3

> *He had seven hundred wives and three hundred concubines. And sure enough, they led his heart away from the LORD.*

Solomon's lust eventually led him not only to promiscuity but also to turning away from God.

WHAT IS THE DIFFERENCE BETWEEN LUST AND LOVE?
2 Samuel 13:14

> *Amnon wouldn't listen to her, and since he was stronger than she was, he raped her.*

Love does not take what is not offered. Lust takes what it wants, regardless of another's needs or desires.

1 Corinthians 13:4-5

> *Love is patient and kind. . . . Love does not demand its own way.*

Love is patient and kind. Lust is impatient and rude.

HOW CAN I KEEP MY DESIRES FROM BECOMING LUST?
Matthew 5:28

> *Anyone who even looks at a woman with lust in his eye has already committed adultery with her in his heart.*

We can prevent lust from taking root in our mind by avoiding that "second look."

Philippians 4:8

> *Think about things that are pure and lovely and admirable.*

When we fill our heart and mind with purity and goodness, lust finds no place to dwell.

Song of Songs 7:6

> *Oh, how delightful you are, my beloved; how pleasant for utter delight!*

God created us to experience the joys of sexual intimacy. Song of Songs reminds us that our pleasure is truly fulfilling only when pursued in accordance with God's standards of marriage, purity, and love.

IS IT POSSIBLE TO LUST FOR SOMETHING OTHER THAN PHYSICAL PLEASURE?

Job 22:24

> *Give up your lust for money, and throw your precious gold into the river.*

Exodus 20:17

> *Do not covet your neighbor's house.*

It is possible to lust for many things. Power, wealth, and material things can all become objects of our lusts.

Lying

WHY DO WE LIE?

Acts 20:30

> *Even some of you will distort the truth in order to draw a following.*

To become popular

Acts 5:2

> [Ananias] brought part of the money to the apostles, but he
> claimed it was the full amount. His wife had agreed to this
> deception.

To make ourselves look good

Genesis 4:9

> The LORD asked Cain, "Where is your brother?". . . "I don't
> know!" Cain retorted.

To avoid punishment

WHY IS IT SO IMPORTANT TO TELL THE TRUTH?

Ephesians 4:25

> Put away all falsehood and "tell your neighbor the truth"
> because we belong to each other.

John 14:6

> Jesus told him, "I am the way, the truth, and the life. No one
> can come to the Father except through me."

God is truth, so lying is in opposition to God. Truth always
seeks what is right and good. Lying always seeks to cover up the
truth.

WHAT DOES GOD THINK ABOUT LYING?

Proverbs 6:16-17

> There are six things the LORD hates—no, seven: . . . haughty
> eyes, a lying tongue.

Proverbs 12:22
> *The LORD hates those who don't keep their word, but he delights in those who do.*

Romans 1:18
> *God shows his anger from heaven against all sinful, wicked people who push the truth away from themselves.*

God *is* truth, so he must hate lies and lying. He cannot tolerate them, because they violate his personhood.

How should I feel about lying?
Psalm 119:163
> *I hate and abhor all falsehood.*

Proverbs 13:5
> *Those who are godly hate lies.*

Colossians 3:9
> *Don't lie to each other, for you have stripped off your old evil nature and all its wicked deeds.*

We should hate lies because they are part of the old sinful nature we had before we were Christians.

Can we lie without using words?
Proverbs 10:18
> *To hide hatred is to be a liar; to slander is to be a fool.*

1 John 1:10
> *If we claim we have not sinned, we are calling God a liar and showing that his word has no place in our hearts.*

We lie whenever we attempt to deceive God, others, or even ourselves.

PROMISE FROM GOD:
Proverbs 12:19

> *Truth stands the test of time; lies are soon exposed.*

WHAT KIND OF RELATIONSHIP SHOULD A MARRIAGE BE?

Genesis 2:18

> *The LORD God said, "It is not good for the man to be alone. I will make a companion who will help him."*

Ecclesiastes 4:9-10

> *Two people can accomplish more than twice as much as one. . . . If one person falls, the other can reach out and help.*

1 Corinthians 11:3

> *There is one thing I want you to know: A man is responsible to Christ, a woman is responsible to her husband, and Christ is responsible to God.*

Matthew 19:4-6

> *"Haven't you read the Scriptures?" Jesus replied. "They record that from the beginning 'God made them male and female.' And he said, 'This explains why a man leaves his father and mother and is joined to his wife, and the two are united into*

> one.' Since they are no longer two but one, let no one separate
> them, for God has joined them together."

Marriage at its best is a relationship so close and intimate that
the two work together as one. It involves mutual trust, mutual
support, mutual defense, mutual comfort, mutual vulnerability,
and mutual responsibility.

WHAT DOES THE BIBLE SAY ABOUT SELECTING A MARRIAGE PARTNER?

Judges 14:3

> *His father and mother objected strenuously, "Isn't there one
> woman in our tribe or among all the Israelites you could marry?
> Why must you go to the pagan Philistines to find a wife?" But
> Samson told his father, "Get her for me. She is the one I want."*

1 Kings 11:2

> *The LORD had clearly instructed his people not to intermarry
> with those nations, because the women they married would lead
> them to worship their gods. Yet Solomon insisted on loving them
> anyway.*

2 Corinthians 6:14

> *Don't team up with those who are unbelievers. How can
> goodness be a partner with wickedness? How can light live with
> darkness?*

God intends marriage to last for life because that is a beautiful
picture of how our relationship with him should also last a
lifetime. When someone is your partner for life, it is so important for that person to share your commitment to God so that
together you can serve him with all your heart.

IS MARRIAGE GOD'S WILL FOR EVERYONE?

Matthew 19:10-12

> Jesus' disciples then said to him, "Then it is better not to
> marry!" "Not everyone can accept this statement," Jesus said.
> "Only those whom God helps. Some are born as eunuchs, some
> have been made that way by others, and some choose not to
> marry for the sake of the Kingdom of Heaven. Let anyone who
> can, accept this statement."

1 Corinthians 7:1-2, 7-9

> Now about the questions you asked in your letter. Yes, it is good
> to live a celibate life. But because there is so much sexual
> immorality, each man should have his own wife, and each
> woman should have her own husband. . . . I wish everyone
> could get along without marrying, just as I do. But we are not
> all the same. God gives some the gift of marriage, and to others
> he gives the gift of singleness. Now I say to those who aren't
> married and to widows—it's better to stay unmarried, just as I
> am. But if they can't control themselves, they should go ahead
> and marry. It's better to marry than to burn with lust.

God created marriage and called it good (see Genesis 2:18-25).
Marriage is also the only way God intended for children to be
born and raised. But the Bible also makes it clear that marriage is
not for everyone.

PROMISE FROM GOD:

Ephesians 5:31

> A man leaves his father and mother and is joined to his wife,
> and the two are united into one.

How do we reach the maturity we desire in life? Who can mentor us along the way?

Psalm 32:8
> *The LORD says, "I will guide you along the best pathway for your life."*

Psalm 92:12
> *The godly will flourish like palm trees.*

Psalm 111:10
> *Reverence for the LORD is the foundation of true wisdom.*

Jeremiah 17:8
> *They are like trees planted along a riverbank, with roots that reach deep into the water.*

Ephesians 3:17
> *I pray that Christ will be more and more at home in your hearts as you trust in him. May your roots go down deep into the soil of God's marvelous love.*

Philippians 1:6
> *I am sure that God, who began the good work within you, will continue his work until it is finally finished.*

Colossians 2:7
> *Let your roots grow down into him and draw up nourishment from him, so you will grow in faith.*

Only God, who created us for a purpose and established the rules for how people relate to each other, can help us find the maturity we desire. Reading the Bible and praying to God are the first and most important steps toward maturity.

1 Corinthians 3:1-2

> *I couldn't talk to you as I would to mature Christians. . . .*
> *I had to feed you with milk and not with solid food.*

1 Corinthians 13:11

> *It's like this: When I was a child, I spoke and thought and*
> *reasoned as a child does. But when I grew up, I put away*
> *childish things.*

Hebrews 6:1

> *Let us stop going over the basics of Christianity again and*
> *again. Let us go on instead and become mature in our*
> *understanding.*

Spiritual growth is like physical growth—we start small and then grow up one day at a time.

WHAT MIGHT KEEP US FROM MATURING AS WE WANT? WHAT MUST WE AVOID?

Isaiah 59:2

> *There is a problem—your sins have cut you off from God.*

2 Timothy 2:4

> *As Christ's soldier, do not let yourself become tied up in the*
> *affairs of this life.*

There are roadblocks to maturing the way we want. Sin is one. Getting distracted by busyness is another. Beware of these roadblocks, for they will keep you from spiritual maturity.

PROMISE FROM GOD:

Philippians 4:13

> *I can do everything with the help of Christ who gives me the strength I need.*

Miracles

WHAT ARE MIRACLES?

Isaiah 41:19-20

> *I will plant trees—cedar, acacia, myrtle, olive, cypress, fir, and pine—on barren land. Everyone will see this miracle and understand that it is the LORD, the Holy One of Israel, who did it.*

Miracles are visible signs that only God can perform that help us know him and see his hand.

HOW DOES GOD USE MIRACLES?

2 Kings 17:36

> *Worship only the LORD, who brought you out of Egypt with such mighty miracles and power. You must worship him and bow before him; offer sacrifices to him alone.*

Daniel 6:27

> *He rescues and saves his people; he performs miraculous signs and wonders in the heavens and on earth. He has rescued Daniel from the power of the lions.*

Micah 7:15

> *"Yes," says the LORD, "I will do mighty miracles for you, like those I did when I rescued you from slavery in Egypt."*

God uses miracles to rescue us.

Exodus 10:1

> *Then the LORD said to Moses, "Return to Pharaoh and again make your demands. I have made him and his officials stubborn so I can continue to display my power by performing miraculous signs among them.*

God uses miracles to demonstrate his power.

Matthew 8:3

> *Jesus touched him. "I want to," he said. "Be healed!" And instantly the leprosy disappeared.*

God uses miracles to show his love for us.

Matthew 14:14

> *A vast crowd was there as he stepped from the boat, and he had compassion on them and healed their sick.*

God uses miracles to show his compassion for us.

HOW SHOULD WE RESPOND WHEN GOD PERFORMS MIRACLES IN OUR LIFE?

Luke 19:37

> *As they reached the place where the road started down from the Mount of Olives, all of his followers began to shout and sing as they walked along, praising God for all the wonderful miracles they had seen.*

We should offer praise and thanksgiving to him.

Psalm 9:1

> *I will thank you, LORD, with all my heart; I will tell of all the marvelous things you have done.*

We can best show our thanks by testifying to what God has done for us.

Mistakes

WHAT DOES THE BIBLE HAVE TO SAY ABOUT MISTAKES?

Genesis 3:12-13

> *"Yes," Adam admitted, "but it was the woman you gave me who brought me the fruit.". . . "The serpent tricked me," she replied.*

Both Adam and Eve responded to mistakes by shifting the blame.

Judges 16:17, 21, 28

> *Finally, Samson told her his secret. . . . So the Philistines*
> *captured him and gouged out his eyes. . . . Then Samson prayed*
> *to the LORD, "Sovereign LORD, remember me again."*

Samson's life, although filled with foolish mistakes, was still
mightily used by God.

James 3:2

> *We all make many mistakes, but those who control their tongues*
> *can also control themselves in every other way.*

One of the most common mistakes is saying something we later
regret.

Jonah 1:3

> *Jonah got up and went in the opposite direction in order to get*
> *away from the LORD.*

The worst mistake we can make is running from God.

Exodus 2:12

> *After looking around to make sure no one was watching, Moses*
> *killed the Egyptian and buried him in the sand.*

Even Moses' life was marred by an immature and terrible
mistake.

Matthew 26:74

> *Peter said, "I swear by God, I don't know the man."*

Christ restored Peter to fellowship even after Peter's most painful mistake.

PROMISE FROM GOD:

Philippians 3:13-14

> *No, dear brothers and sisters, I am still not all I should be, but I am focusing all my energies on this one thing: Forgetting the past and looking forward to what lies ahead I strain to reach the end of the race and receive the prize for which God, through Christ Jesus, is calling us up to heaven.*

Modesty

WHAT IS THE IMPORTANCE OF MODESTY?

1 Timothy 2:15

> *Women will be saved through childbearing and by continuing to live in faith, love, holiness, and modesty.*

1 Peter 2:12

> *Be careful how you live among your unbelieving neighbors. Even if they accuse you of doing wrong, they will see your honorable behavior, and they will believe and give honor to God when he comes to judge the world.*

1 Peter 3.1-2

> *In the same way, you wives must accept the authority of your husbands, even those who refuse to accept the Good News. Your godly lives will speak to them better than any words. They will be won over by watching your pure, godly behavior.*

Godly modesty is setting an example of appropriateness that cannot be criticized. Modesty can win over people who might otherwise be antagonistic.

HOW CAN I BE MODEST IN MY APPEARANCE?

1 Timothy 2.9

> *I want women to be modest in their appearance. They should wear decent and appropriate clothing and not draw attention to themselves.*

1 Corinthians 6.19

> *Don't you know that your body is the temple of the Holy Spirit, who lives in you and was given to you by God? You do not belong to yourself.*

1 Peter 3.3-4

> *Don't be concerned about the outward beauty that depends on fancy hairstyles, expensive jewelry, or beautiful clothes. You should be known for the beauty that comes from within, the unfading beauty of a gentle and quiet spirit, which is so precious to God.*

Modesty focuses on inward beauty, for that kind of beauty remains strong and youthful long after our body turns old and frail.

HOW SHOULD I SHOW MODESTY IN MY BEHAVIOR?

Romans 13:13

> *We should be decent and true in everything we do, so that everyone can approve of our behavior. Don't participate in wild parties and getting drunk, or in adultery and immoral living, or in fighting and jealousy.*

Ephesians 5:8

> *Though your hearts were once full of darkness, now you are full of light from the Lord, and your behavior should show it!*

Titus 2:12

> *We are instructed to turn from godless living and sinful pleasures. We should live in this evil world with self-control, right conduct, and devotion to God.*

We can show modesty by living with self-control, avoiding indecent behavior, devoting ourselves to God, and shining Christ's light in a dark world.

PROMISE FROM GOD:

1 Peter 2:12

> *Be careful how you live among your unbelieving neighbors. Even if they accuse you of doing wrong, they will see your honorable behavior, and they will believe and give honor to God when he comes to judge the world.*

WHAT IS A PROPER PERSPECTIVE TOWARD MONEY?

Psalm 23:1

> *The LORD is my shepherd; I have everything I need.*

Matthew 6:24

> *No one can serve two masters. . . . You cannot serve both God and money.*

Money cannot satisfy our deepest needs. We must keep reminding ourselves that God must be first in our life.

Psalm 119:36

> *Give me an eagerness for your decrees; do not inflict me with love for money!*

1 Timothy 6:10

> *The love of money is at the root of all kinds of evil.*

Hebrews 13:5

> *Stay away from the love of money; be satisfied with what you have. For God has said, "I will never fail you. I will never forsake you."*

Money is not the root of all kinds of evil—the *love* of it is!

Proverbs 11:28
> *Trust in your money and down you go!*

Isaiah 55:2
> *Why spend your money on food that does not give you strength? . . . Listen, and I will tell you where to get food that is good for the soul!*

Too often we buy things to fill a void or an emotional need in our life. The Bible points to a way to acquire deep and lasting happiness that always satisfies.

Proverbs 19:1
> *It is better to be poor and honest than to be a fool and dishonest.*

Mark 8:36
> *How do you benefit if you gain the whole world but lose your own soul in the process?*

No amount of money is worth being gained deceptively or dishonestly. Taking advantage of others to make money is stealing. Those who do this lose far more than they could ever gain.

Philippians 4:11-12
> *I have learned how to get along happily whether I have much or little. . . . I have learned the secret of living in every situation.*

Philippians 4:19
> *This same God who takes care of me will supply all your needs from his glorious riches.*

The Bible promises that God will supply all of our needs. The problem comes when our definition of "need" is different from God's. The first thing we must do is study God's word to discover what he says we need for a fulfilling life.

Mark 12:43-44

> *He called his disciples to him and said, "I assure you, this poor widow has given more than all the others have given."*

1 John 3:17

> *If anyone has enough money to live well and sees a brother or sister in need and refuses to help—how can God's love be in that person?*

Consistently and generously giving away our money might be the most effective way to keep us from loving it. When we see what giving does in the life of others, we experience a satisfaction that material possessions could never generate. This kind of giving is a measure of our Christian love.

Proverbs 3:9-10

> *Honor the LORD with your wealth and with the best part of everything your land produces. Then he will fill your barns with grain.*

Malachi 3:10

> *"Bring all the tithes into the storehouse. . . . If you do," says the LORD Almighty, "I will open the windows of heaven for you."*

Instead of viewing money as ours, to use as we wish, we should view it as God's, to use as *he* wishes. Giving God the first part of everything we receive will help us maintain this perspective.

2 Corinthians 9:6
> *The one who plants generously will get a generous crop.*

Proverbs 21:20
> *Fools spend whatever they get.*

Proverbs 28:19
> *Hard workers have plenty of food.*

Matthew 25:14
> *He called together his servants and gave them money to invest for him while he was gone.*

1 Corinthians 4:12
> *We have worked wearily with our own hands to earn our living.*

Luke 6:38
> *If you give, you will receive.*

God commands us to be good stewards in earning, spending, and saving our money. He understands the importance of providing for the needs of our family and the future. But he also expects us to use our money generously to help others.

WHY DO WE ALWAYS SEEM TO WANT TO ACCUMULATE MORE?

Ecclesiastes 10:19
> *A party gives laughter, and wine gives happiness, and money gives everything!*

Money can get us many things in the world. That is why we desire it.

Mark 10.22

> At this, the man's face fell, and he went sadly away because he had many possessions.

We accumulate money because we trust money and wealth to bring us happiness. How much more happy and productive we could be if we set our mind to accumulating treasure in heaven!

WHY DON'T I EVER SEEM TO HAVE ENOUGH?
Isaiah 55.2

> Why spend your money on food that does not give you strength?

We don't have enough when we foolishly waste our money on what does not satisfy the soul.

Haggai 1.4

> Why are you living in luxurious houses while my house lies in ruins?

We don't have enough when we don't manage our money according to God's priorities.

Luke 12.15

> Don't be greedy for what you don't have. Real life is not measured by how much we own.

If we depend on our wealth to bring security, there will never be enough.

IS DEBT A SIN?

Proverbs 22:7

> Just as the rich rule the poor, so the borrower is servant to the lender.

It is wise to avoid borrowing money.

Proverbs 6:1-3

> If you co-sign a loan for a friend or guarantee the debt of someone you hardly know . . . get out of it if you possibly can!

Debt is a dangerous thing. We should avoid it whenever possible.

Romans 13:8

> Pay all your debts.

Failing to repay a debt is clearly sinful.

PROMISE FROM GOD:

Matthew 6:31-33

> Don't worry about having enough food or drink or clothing. Why be like the pagans who are so deeply concerned about these things? Your heavenly Father already knows all your needs, and he will give you all you need from day to day if you live for him and make the Kingdom of God your primary concern.

Motives

DOES GOD CARE ABOUT OUR MOTIVES?

1 Chronicles 29:17

> I know, my God, that you examine our hearts and rejoice when
> you find integrity there. You know I have done all this with
> good motives, and I have watched your people offer their gifts
> willingly and joyously.

Proverbs 20:27

> The LORD's searchlight penetrates the human spirit, exposing
> every hidden motive.

Proverbs 21:27

> God loathes the sacrifice of an evil person, especially when it is
> brought with ulterior motives.

Our motives are very important to God.

1 Samuel 16:7

> But the LORD said to Samuel, "Don't judge by his appearance
> or height, for I have rejected him. The LORD doesn't make
> decisions the way you do! People judge by outward appearance,
> but the LORD looks at a person's thoughts and intentions."

God puts more importance on our motives than on our
appearance or outward actions.

James 4:3

> *When you do ask, you don't get it because your whole motive is wrong—you want only what will give you pleasure.*

Wrong motives can hinder our prayers.

Philippians 1:17-18

> *Those others do not have pure motives as they preach about Christ. They preach with selfish ambition, not sincerely, intending to make my chains more painful to me. But whether or not their motives are pure, the fact remains that the message about Christ is being preached, so I rejoice. And I will continue to rejoice.*

Even when our motives are wrong, God can use us for good.

How can I have motives that please God?

1 Chronicles 28:9-10

> *Solomon, my son, get to know the God of your ancestors. Worship and serve him with your whole heart and with a willing mind. For the LORD sees every heart and understands and knows every plan and thought. If you seek him, you will find him. But if you forsake him, he will reject you forever. So take this seriously.*

Worshiping and serving God with our whole heart and mind can give us right motives.

Psalm 19:14

> *May the words of my mouth and the thoughts of my heart be pleasing to you, O LORD, my rock and my redeemer.*

Ask God to give you motives that please him.

Psalm 26:2

Put me on trial, LORD, and cross-examine me. Test my motives and affections.

Proverbs 17:3

Fire tests the purity of silver and gold, but the LORD tests the heart.

God will test our motives, giving us an opportunity to grow.

PROMISE FROM GOD:

Ezekiel 36:26

I will give you a new heart with new and right desires, and I will put a new spirit in you. I will take out your stony heart of sin and give you a new, obedient heart.

Music

DOES GOD LIKE MUSIC?

2 Chronicles 5:13-14

The trumpeters and singers performed together in unison to praise and give thanks to the LORD. Accompanied by trumpets, cymbals, and other instruments, they raised their voices and praised the LORD with these words: "He is so good! His faithful love endures forever!" At that moment a cloud filled the Temple of the LORD. The priests could not continue their work because the glorious presence of the LORD filled the Temple of God.

God likes music—he came with his powerful presence and entered the temple during a time of musical worship.

Zephaniah 3:17

The LORD your God has arrived to live among you. . . . He will exult over you by singing a happy song.

God created music—he himself is the singer!

Psalm 147:1

How good it is to sing praises to our God! How delightful and how right!

God delights when we use music to praise him.

WHAT ROLE DOES MUSIC HAVE IN WORSHIP?

2 Chronicles 23:13

The officers and trumpeters were surrounding him, and people from all over the land were rejoicing and blowing trumpets. Singers with musical instruments were leading the people in a great celebration.

Throughout Scripture, music was used in worshiping the Lord.

Psalm 81:2-4

Sing! Beat the tambourine. Play the sweet lyre and the harp. Sound the trumpet for a sacred feast when the moon is new, when the moon is full. For this is required by the laws of Israel; it is a law of the God of Jacob.

David saw music as a required form of worship.

ARE THERE TYPES OF MUSIC THAT WE SHOULD STAY AWAY FROM?

Philippians 4:8

> *Now, dear brothers and sisters, let me say one more thing as I close this letter. Fix your thoughts on what is true and honorable and right. Think about things that are pure and lovely and admirable. Think about things that are excellent and worthy of praise.*

As Christians, we should protect our mind from things that are not pure. We should avoid music that leads us to think about untrue, dishonorable, unadmirable, unlovely, or impure things.

PROMISE FROM GOD:

Isaiah 51:11

> *Those who have been ransomed by the LORD will return to Jerusalem, singing songs of everlasting joy. Sorrow and mourning will disappear, and they will be overcome with joy and gladness.*

Obedience

IS OBEDIENCE TO GOD REALLY NECESSARY SINCE WE ARE SAVED BY FAITH?

Deuteronomy 10:12-13

> *Now, Israel, what does the LORD your God require of you? He requires you to fear him, to live according to his will, to love*

*and worship him with all your heart and soul, and to obey the
LORD's commands and laws that I am giving you today for
your own good.*

Philippians 2:12

*Dearest friends, you were always so careful to follow my instruc-
tions when I was with you. And now that I am away you must
be even more careful to put into action God's saving work in
your lives, obeying God with deep reverence and fear.*

Obedience is putting into action God's saving work in our life.

Jeremiah 7:23

*Obey me, and I will be your God, and you will be my people.
Only do as I say, and all will be well!*

Obedience to God is an essential element of our relationship
with him.

Hebrews 11:8

It was by faith that Abraham obeyed.

Obedience is an act of faith.

Romans 1:5

*Through Christ, God has given us the privilege and authority to
tell Gentiles everywhere what God has done for them, so that
they will believe and obey him, bringing glory to his name.*

Romans 6:17

*Thank God! Once you were slaves of sin, but now you have
obeyed with all your heart the new teaching God has given you.*

Putting our trust in God for salvation through Christ is equivalent to obeying his message of the Good News.

Titus 1:16

> *Such people claim they know God, but they deny him by the way they live. They are despicable and disobedient, worthless for doing anything good.*

If we are consistently disobedient to God, our claim that we know him is meaningless.

Leviticus 9:6

> *Moses told them, "When you have followed these instructions from the LORD, the glorious presence of the LORD will appear to you."*

IN WHAT WAYS DOES GOD WANT US TO OBEY HIM?

Genesis 6:22

> *Noah did everything exactly as God had commanded him.*

Deuteronomy 5:32

> *You must obey all the commands of the LORD your God, following his instructions in every detail.*

God wants us to do everything he commands us to do.

1 Samuel 15:22

> *Samuel replied, "What is more pleasing to the LORD: your burnt offerings and sacrifices or your obedience to his voice? Obedience is far better than sacrifice. Listening to him is much better than offering the fat of rams."*

Obedience to God involves listening to what he says.

Exodus 12:28

> The people of Israel did just as the LORD had commanded through Moses and Aaron.

Romans 13:1

> Obey the government, for God is the one who put it there. All governments have been placed in power by God.

Hebrews 13:17

> Obey your spiritual leaders and do what they say.

God shows us through human authorities what he wants us to do.

Exodus 1:17

> Because the midwives feared God, they refused to obey the king and allowed the boys to live, too.

Acts 4:19-20

> Peter and John replied, "Do you think God wants us to obey you rather than him? We cannot stop telling about the wonderful things we have seen and heard."

Acts 5:29

> Peter and the apostles replied, "We must obey God rather than human authority."

We must obey God over human authorities.

PROMISE FROM GOD:

James 1:25

> If you keep looking steadily into God's perfect law—the law that sets you free—and if you do what it says and don't forget what you heard, then God will bless you for doing it.

Opportunities

HOW SHOULD I RESPOND TO OPPORTUNITIES?

Genesis 40:8

> They replied, "We both had dreams last night, but there is no one here to tell us what they mean." "Interpreting dreams is God's business," Joseph replied. "Tell me what you saw."

Ephesians 5:16

> Make the most of every opportunity for doing good in these evil days.

Philippians 1:14

> Because of my imprisonment, many of the Christians here have gained confidence and become more bold in telling others about Christ.

Seize opportunities to do good, even when you are experiencing personal hardship!

Proverbs 1:24-27

I called you so often, but you didn't come. I reached out to you, but you paid no attention. You ignored my advice and rejected the correction I offered. So I will laugh when you are in trouble! I will mock you when disaster overtakes you—when calamity overcomes you like a storm, when you are engulfed by trouble, and when anguish and distress overwhelm you.

Jeremiah 13:16

Give glory to the LORD your God before it is too late. Acknowledge him before he brings darkness upon you, causing you to stumble and fall on the dark mountains.

Respond to God's call, and get to know him and his truth while there is opportunity.

Proverbs 12:11

Hard work means prosperity; only fools idle away their time.

John 9:4

All of us must quickly carry out the tasks assigned us by the one who sent me, because there is little time left before the night falls and all work comes to an end.

When an opportunity presents itself, respond by acting quickly and working hard.

1 Corinthians 16:8-9

In the meantime, I will be staying here at Ephesus until the Festival of Pentecost, for there is a wide-open door for a great work here, and many people are responding.

Be willing to change your plans in order to take advantage of an opportunity.

Ezekiel 33.3-6

> *When the watchman sees the enemy coming, he blows the alarm to warn the people. Then if those who hear the alarm refuse to take action—well, it is their own fault if they die. . . . But if the watchman sees the enemy coming and doesn't sound the alarm to warn the people, he is responsible for their deaths.*

Acts 11.19-21

> *The believers who had fled from Jerusalem during the persecution after Stephen's death traveled as far as Phoenicia, Cyprus, and Antioch of Syria. They preached the Good News, but only to Jews. However, some of the believers who went to Antioch from Cyprus and Cyrene began preaching to Gentiles about the Lord Jesus. The power of the Lord was upon them, and large numbers of these Gentiles believed and turned to the Lord.*

Take every opportunity to warn people of God's judgment and to proclaim the Good News of Christ's salvation.

How do I prepare for opportunities before they come?

Matthew 9.37

> *He said to his disciples, "The harvest is so great, but the workers are so few."*

Pray that God will supply enough people to respond to the opportunities that become available.

Matthew 25:1-13

The Kingdom of Heaven can be illustrated by the story of ten bridesmaids who took their lamps and went to meet the bridegroom. Five of them were foolish, and five were wise. The five who were foolish took no oil for their lamps, but the other five were wise enough to take along extra oil. When the bridegroom was delayed, they all lay down and slept. At midnight they were roused by the shout, "Look, the bridegroom is coming! Come out and welcome him!" All the bridesmaids got up and prepared their lamps. Then the five foolish ones asked the others, "Please give us some of your oil because our lamps are going out." But the others replied, "We don't have enough for all of us. Go to a shop and buy some for yourselves." But while they were gone to buy oil, the bridegroom came, and those who were ready went in with him to the marriage feast, and the door was locked. Later, when the other five bridesmaids returned, they stood outside, calling, "Sir, open the door for us!" But he called back, "I don't know you!" So stay awake and be prepared.

Stay awake and be prepared for Christ's coming.

Matthew 26:40-41

Couldn't you stay awake and watch with me even one hour? Keep alert and pray. Otherwise temptation will overpower you. For though the spirit is willing enough, the body is weak!

Always be alert and prayerful in order to respond properly to every situation.

John 12:35

> Jesus replied, "My light will shine out for you just a little while longer. Walk in it while you can, so you will not stumble when the darkness falls."

Walking in Christ's light will help us to be ready for opportunities.

PROMISES FROM GOD:

Matthew 25:29

> To those who use well what they are given, even more will be given, and they will have an abundance. But from those who are unfaithful, even what little they have will be taken away.

Revelation 3:8

> I know all the things you do, and I have opened a door for you that no one can shut.

Parents

HOW SHOULD WE TREAT OUR PARENTS?

Exodus 20:12

> Honor your father and mother. Then you will live a long, full life in the land the LORD your God will give you.

Mark 7:12-13

> You let them disregard their needy parents. As such, you break the law of God in order to protect your own tradition. And this is only one example. There are many, many others.

Ephesians 6:1

> *Children, obey your parents because you belong to the Lord, for this is the right thing to do.*

Even if we disagree with our parents, we must still show them honor, respect, and obedience.

Promise from God:

Ephesians 6:3

> *This is the promise: If you honor your father and mother, "you will live a long life, full of blessing."*

Patience

How can I grow in patience?

Psalm 40:1

> *I waited patiently for the LORD to help me, and he turned to me and heard my cry.*

We must wait patiently in prayer for God to do his work in us.

Habakkuk 2:3

> *If it seems slow, wait patiently, for it will surely take place. It will not be delayed.*

We develop patience as we learn to live from an eternal perspective.

Galatians 5:22

> *When the Holy Spirit controls our lives, he will produce this kind of fruit in us: love, joy, peace, patience.*

Patience is a by-product of the presence and work of the Holy Spirit in our heart.

1 Corinthians 13:4

> *Love is patient and kind.*

Patience is one of the evidences of love.

Romans 8:25

> *If we look forward to something we don't have yet, we must wait patiently and confidently.*

Patience is produced by a believer's hope in God's eternal glory.

PROMISE FROM GOD:

Lamentations 3:25

> *The LORD is wonderfully good to those who wait for him and seek him.*

Peer Pressure

Is all peer pressure bad?

James 4:17

> *Remember, it is sin to know what you ought to do and then not do it.*

Good peer pressure will hold you accountable for the things God calls you to do.

How do I tell the difference between good and bad peer pressure?

Matthew 7:20

> *Yes, the way to identify a tree or a person is by the kind of fruit that is produced.*

Good peer pressure will encourage you toward living a more godly life, while bad peer pressure will lead you away from godly living.

How can we resist peer pressure?

Matthew 1:24

> *When Joseph woke up, he did what the angel of the Lord commanded. He brought Mary home to be his wife.*

Joseph provides an excellent example for us. His friends would have advised him to break off the engagement immediately. However, Joseph chose to obey God rather than people.

Luke 20:21

> They said, "Teacher, we know that you speak and teach what is right and are not influenced by what others think. You sincerely teach the ways of God."

It is easier to resist bad influences when you are grounded in God's Word.

PROMISE FROM GOD:

1 Corinthians 10:13

> Remember that the temptations that come into your life are no different from what others experience. And God is faithful. He will keep the temptation from becoming so strong that you can't stand up against it. When you are tempted, he will show you a way out so that you will not give in to it.

Persecution

WHY DO CHRISTIANS EXPERIENCE PERSECUTION?

John 15:20-21

> Since they persecuted me, naturally they will persecute you. And if they had listened to me, they would listen to you! The people of the world will hate you because you belong to me.

Galatians 5:11

> *The fact that I am still being persecuted proves that I am still preaching salvation.*

Many people don't want good and right to win over evil. Those who oppose God and what is good will persecute Christians. In many cases, persecution is a sign that you are making a real difference for Christ.

IF GOD HAS A PLAN FOR MY LIFE, WHAT IS THE PURPOSE OF PERSECUTION?

2 Thessalonians 1:5

> *God will use this persecution to show his justice. For he will make you worthy of his Kingdom, for which you are suffering.*

Persecution defines who we are going to be in Christ. We grow as we respond to persecution in a godly way.

WHEN WE EXPERIENCE PERSECUTION, WHAT ARE WE SUPPOSED TO DO?

Matthew 5:44

> *Love your enemies! Pray for those who persecute you!*

Romans 12:14

> *If people persecute you because you are a Christian, don't curse them; pray that God will bless them.*

We are to pray that God will bless those who persecute us, for it may be through our response to persecution that God will touch a hard heart.

Revelation 14:12

> *Let this encourage God's holy people to endure persecution patiently and remain firm to the end, obeying his commands and trusting in Jesus.*

Matthew 27:12

> *When the leading priests and other leaders made their accusations against him, Jesus remained silent.*

We are to remain obedient to God and endure the persecution patiently, just as Jesus did when he was persecuted.

PROMISE FROM GOD:

Matthew 5:11-12

> *God blesses you when you are mocked and persecuted and lied about because you are my followers. Be happy about it! Be very glad! For a great reward awaits you in heaven.*

Planning

WHY SHOULD I PLAN AHEAD?

Genesis 41:28, 33, 36

> *This will happen just as I have described it, for God has shown you what he is about to do. . . . My suggestion is that you find the wisest man in Egypt and put him in charge of a nationwide program. . . . That way there will be enough to eat when the seven years of famine come. Otherwise disaster will surely strike the land, and all the people will die.*

Proverbs 13:16
> Wise people think before they act; fools don't and even brag
> about it!

Proverbs 14:8
> The wise look ahead to see what is coming, but fools deceive
> themselves.

Proverbs 22:3
> A prudent person foresees the danger ahead and takes
> precautions; the simpleton goes blindly on and suffers the
> consequences.

Planning and foresight will help us prepare for danger ahead so
that we can avoid disastrous consequences.

Proverbs 20:4
> If you are too lazy to plow in the right season, you will have no
> food at the harvest.

Luke 14:28
> Don't begin until you count the cost. For who would begin
> construction of a building without first getting estimates and
> then checking to see if there is enough money to pay the bills?

Planning is a necessary part of living.

How do I go about planning ahead?
Exodus 25:40
> Be sure that you make everything according to the pattern
> I have shown you here on the mountain.

Exodus 26.30

> *Set up this Tabernacle according to the design you were shown on the mountain.*

Follow God's revealed will when you make your plans.

Genesis 11.4

> *Let's build a great city with a tower that reaches to the skies— a monument to our greatness! This will bring us together and keep us from scattering all over the world.*

Don't make plans that conflict with God's revealed will.

1 Chronicles 28.19

> *"Every part of this plan," David told Solomon, "was given to me in writing from the hand of the LORD."*

Proverbs 3.5-6

> *Trust in the LORD with all your heart; do not depend on your own understanding. Seek his will in all you do, and he will direct your paths.*

As we seek God, he will guide us in making our plans.

Isaiah 14.26-27

> *I have a plan for the whole earth, for my mighty power reaches throughout the world. The LORD Almighty has spoken—who can change his plans? When his hand moves, who can stop him?*

Romans 8:28
> *We know that God causes everything to work together for the good of those who love God and are called according to his purpose for them.*

God will work through our plans, and in spite of them, to accomplish his ends.

PROMISES FROM GOD:

Proverbs 19:21
> *You can make many plans, but the LORD's purpose will prevail.*

Ephesians 1:9-10
> *God's secret plan has now been revealed to us; it is a plan centered on Christ, designed long ago according to his good pleasure. And this is his plan: At the right time he will bring everything together under the authority of Christ—everything in heaven and on earth.*

Poor

DOESN'T GOD CARE THAT I'M POOR? I FEEL SO LONELY WHEN I REALIZE HOW SO MANY OTHERS SEEM TO HAVE ALL THEY NEED WHILE I'M STRUGGLING.

Isaiah 25:4
> *To the poor, O LORD, you are a refuge from the storm . . . a shelter from the rain and the heat.*

Matthew 8.20

> *Jesus said, "Foxes have dens to live in, and birds have nests, but I, the Son of Man, have no home of my own, not even a place to lay my head."*

Romans 8.35-37

> *Does it mean [God] no longer loves us if we have trouble or calamity, or are persecuted, or are hungry or cold or in danger or threatened with death? . . . No . . . overwhelming victory is ours through Christ, who loved us.*

God knows what poverty is like—Christ himself was homeless! God cares and will be our refuge, even as we experience poverty.

DOES GOD REALLY CARE ABOUT THE POOR?

Psalm 35.10

> *Who else rescues the weak and helpless from the strong? Who else protects the poor and needy from those who want to rob them?*

Psalm 40.17

> *I am poor and needy, but the Lord is thinking about me right now.*

Psalm 72.12

> *He will rescue the poor when they cry to him; he will help the oppressed, who have no one to defend them.*

Psalm 102.17

> *He will listen to the prayers of the destitute. He will not reject their pleas.*

Psalm 113.6-8

> *Far below him are the heavens and the earth. He stoops to look, and he lifts the poor from the dirt and the needy from the garbage dump. He sets them among princes.*

God cares deeply for the poor, and he commands all believers to care for them too.

WHAT IS MY RESPONSIBILITY TO THE POOR?

Leviticus 25:39

If any of your Israelite relatives go bankrupt and sell themselves to you, do not treat them as slaves.

Proverbs 19:17

If you help the poor, you are lending to the LORD—and he will repay you!

Proverbs 22:9

Blessed are those who are generous, because they feed the poor.

Isaiah 58:10

Feed the hungry and help those in trouble. Then your light will shine out from the darkness, and the darkness around you will be as bright as day.

Matthew 7:12

Do for others what you would like them to do for you.

James 2:9

If you pay special attention to the rich, you are committing a sin.

God has compassion for the poor, so if we would be godly, *we* must have compassion for the poor. Compassion that does not reach into our checkbooks or onto our "to do" list is theoretical compassion, not real godly compassion. Helping the poor is not merely an obligation but a privilege that can bring us great joy.

PROMISE FROM GOD:

2 Corinthians 8:9

> *You know how full of love and kindness our Lord Jesus Christ was. Though he was very rich, yet for your sakes he became poor, so that by his poverty he could make you rich.*

Popularity

WHAT DOES THE BIBLE SAY ABOUT BEING POPULAR?

Galatians 1:10

> *Obviously, I'm not trying to be a people pleaser! No, I am trying to please God. If I were still trying to please people, I would not be Christ's servant.*

The Bible cautions us about our motives for wanting to be popular. If we are trying to please people more than God, then we are not effectively serving him, and we have misplaced priorities.

HOW SHOULD WE RESPOND TO SOMEONE ELSE'S POPULARITY?

John 3:26-27, 30

> *John's disciples came to him and said, "Teacher, the man you met on the other side of the Jordan River, the one you said was the Messiah, is also baptizing people. And everybody is going over there instead of coming here to us." John replied, "God in heaven appoints each person's work. . . . He must become greater and greater, and I must become less and less."*

Popularity can lead to pride. John the Baptist understood that he had a job to do for God—he did not worry about his own popularity. By contrast, his disciples wrongly became jealous over who was baptizing more people.

WHAT ARE SOME OF THE TRAPS OF WANTING TO BE POPULAR?
Esther 3.2
> *All the king's officials would bow down before Haman to show him respect whenever he passed by, for so the king had commanded. But Mordecai refused to bow down or show him respect.*

We should avoid popularity when it causes us to disown or disobey God.

John 12.43
> *They loved human praise more than the praise of God.*

We should avoid popularity when we recognize that our love for popularity is greater than our love for God.

PROMISE FROM GOD:
Matthew 23.12
> *Those who exalt themselves will be humbled, and those who humble themselves will be exalted.*

WHAT IS PRAYER?

2 Chronicles 7:14

> *If my people who are called by my name will humble themselves
> and pray and seek my face and turn from their wicked ways, I
> will hear from heaven.*

Prayer is an act of humble worship in which we seek God with
all our heart.

Psalm 38:18

> *I confess my sins; I am deeply sorry for what I have done.*

Prayer often begins with a confession of sin.

1 Samuel 14:36

> *The priest said, "Let's ask God first."*

2 Samuel 5:19

> *David asked the LORD, "Should I go out to fight the
> Philistines?"*

Prayer is asking God for guidance and waiting for his direction
and leading.

Mark 1:35

> *The next morning Jesus awoke long before daybreak and went out alone into the wilderness to pray.*

Prayer is an expression of an intimate relationship with our heavenly Father, who makes his own love and resources available to us.

Psalm 9:1-2

> *I will thank you, LORD, with all my heart. . . . I will sing praises to your name, O Most High.*

Through prayer we praise our mighty God.

DOES THE BIBLE TEACH A "RIGHT" WAY TO PRAY?

Nehemiah 1:4

> *For days I mourned, fasted, and prayed to the God of heaven.*

Throughout the Bible effective prayer includes elements of adoration, confession, and commitment, as well as requests.

Matthew 6:9

> *Pray like this.*

Jesus taught his disciples that true prayer is the result of an intimate relationship with the Father and includes a dependency for daily needs, commitment to obedience, and forgiveness of sin.

Luke 18:1

> *One day Jesus told his disciples a story to illustrate their need for constant prayer and to show them that they must never give up.*

Prayer is to be consistent and persistent.

Does God always answer prayer?

James 5:16

> Confess your sins to each other and pray for each other so that you may be healed. The earnest prayer of a righteous person has great power and wonderful results.

1 John 5:14

> We can be confident that he will listen to us whenever we ask him for anything in line with his will.

We can be confident that God will respond to our prayer when we submit to his will.

2 Corinthians 12:8-9

> Three different times I begged the Lord to take it away. Each time he said, ". . . My power works best in your weakness."

Sometimes, like Paul, we find that God answers prayer by giving us not what we ask for but something better.

Exodus 14:15

> The LORD said to Moses, "Why are you crying out to me? Tell the people to get moving!"

Our prayer must be accompanied by a willingness to obey with our actions.

PROMISE FROM GOD:

1 Peter 3:12

> The eyes of the Lord watch over those who do right, and his ears are open to their prayers.

Preparation

HOW DO I PREPARE FOR THE IMPORTANT EVENTS IN MY LIFE?

Genesis 14:14-16

> When Abram learned that Lot had been captured, he called together the men born into his household, 318 of them in all. He chased after Kedorlaomer's army until he caught up with them in Dan. There he divided his men and attacked during the night from several directions. Kedorlaomer's army fled, but Abram chased them to Hobah, north of Damascus. Abram and his allies recovered everything—the goods that had been taken, Abram's nephew Lot with his possessions, and all the women and other captives.

Genesis 41:14

> Pharaoh sent for Joseph at once, and he was brought hastily from the dungeon. After a quick shave and change of clothes, he went in and stood in Pharaoh's presence.

Sometimes we can't prepare in advance for what will happen, so swift action and decision making are sometimes necessary.

Numbers 27.15-17

> Moses said to the LORD, "O LORD, the God of the spirits of all living things, please appoint a new leader for the community. Give them someone who will lead them into battle, so the people of the LORD will not be like sheep without a shepherd."

Looking ahead at what is coming will often show us what needs to be done before the moment arrives.

Joshua 3.5

> Joshua told the people, "Purify yourselves, for tomorrow the LORD will do great wonders among you."

2 Timothy 2.21

> If you keep yourself pure, you will be a utensil God can use for his purpose. Your life will be clean, and you will be ready for the Master to use you for every good work.

Purity not only prepares us for the coming of Christ, but it also prepares us to serve God and be involved in the wonderful things he is doing.

1 Corinthians 11.27-28

> If anyone eats this bread or drinks this cup of the Lord unworthily, that person is guilty of sinning against the body and the blood of the Lord. That is why you should examine yourself before eating the bread and drinking from the cup.

We should prepare for worship by examining and purifying ourselves.

Ephesians 6:10-12

A final word: Be strong with the Lord's mighty power. Put on all of God's armor so that you will be able to stand firm against all strategies and tricks of the Devil. For we are not fighting against people made of flesh and blood, but against the evil rulers and authorities of the unseen world, against those mighty powers of darkness who rule this world, and against wicked spirits in the heavenly realms.

Prepare for spiritual conflict by "putting on" truth, righteousness, knowledge of the Good News of Christ and of God's Word in general, faith, assurance of salvation, and prayer.

1 Peter 3:15

You must worship Christ as Lord of your life. And if you are asked about your Christian hope, always be ready to explain it.

We must always be ready to explain the Good News about Christ.

Luke 21:14-15

Don't worry about how to answer the charges against you, for I will give you the right words and such wisdom that none of your opponents will be able to reply!

We must prepare for spiritual conflict, but when it comes, we can trust God to work through us by his Holy Spirit.

Matthew 3:2

Turn from your sins and turn to God, because the Kingdom of Heaven is near.

1 Peter 1:13-15

Think clearly and exercise self-control. Look forward to the special blessings that will come to you at the return of Jesus Christ. Obey God because you are his children. Don't slip back into your old ways of doing evil; you didn't know any better then. But now you must be holy in everything you do, just as God—who chose you to be his children—is holy.

We prepare for the coming of Christ by turning away from sin, turning to God in faith, and purifying our life with humility and holiness before God.

PROMISE FROM GOD:

Matthew 5:8

God blesses those whose hearts are pure, for they will see God.

John 14:2-3

There are many rooms in my Father's home, and I am going to prepare a place for you. If this were not so, I would tell you plainly. When everything is ready, I will come and get you, so that you will always be with me where I am.

Priorities

WHAT SHOULD BE MY HIGHEST PRIORITY?

Mark 12:29-30

Jesus replied, "The most important commandment is this:

> 'Hear, O Israel! The Lord our God is the one and only Lord.
> And you must love the Lord your God with all your heart, all
> your soul, all your mind, and all your strength.'"

The priority of priorities is to love God.

HOW CAN I DEVELOP THE RIGHT PRIORITIES?

Proverbs 3:5-6

> Trust in the LORD with all your heart; do not depend on your
> own understanding. Seek his will in all you do, and he will
> direct your paths.

1 Kings 3:9

> Give me an understanding mind so that I can govern your
> people well and know the difference between right and wrong.
> For who by himself is able to govern this great nation of yours?

1 Samuel 14:36

> Then Saul said, "Let's chase the Philistines all night and destroy
> every last one of them." His men replied, "We'll do whatever
> you think is best." But the priest said, "Let's ask God first."

Matthew 8:22

> Jesus told him, "Follow me now! Let those who are spiritually
> dead care for their own dead."

Seeking God and doing his will should be our first priority and
will help put all of our other priorities in order.

WHAT ARE SOME OF THE BENEFITS OF LIVING BY RIGHT PRIORITIES, AND WHAT ARE THE DANGERS OF LIVING BY WRONG PRIORITIES?

Psalm 128:1-4

> How happy are those who fear the LORD—all who follow his ways! You will enjoy the fruit of your labor. How happy you will be! How rich your life! Your wife will be like a fruitful vine, flourishing within your home. And look at all those children! There they sit around your table as vigorous and healthy as young olive trees. That is the LORD's reward for those who fear him.

Proverbs 14:26

> Those who fear the LORD are secure; he will be a place of refuge for their children.

Right priorities bring true happiness, joy, delight, and an abundant life.

Psalm 127:1-2

> Unless the LORD builds a house, the work of the builders is useless. Unless the LORD protects a city, guarding it with sentries will do no good. It is useless for you to work so hard from early morning until late at night, anxiously working for food to eat; for God gives rest to his loved ones.

Wrong priorities can lead to useless activity and unproductive anxiety—both a fruitless waste of life.

WHAT SHOULD BE MY PRIORITY CONCERNING THE PURSUIT OF KNOWLEDGE?

1 Corinthians 8:1-3

You think that everyone should agree with your perfect knowledge. While knowledge may make us feel important, it is love that really builds up the church. Anyone who claims to know all the answers doesn't really know very much. But the person who loves God is the one God knows and cares for.

Treating others with Christ's love is more important than acquiring knowledge.

WHAT SHOULD BE MY PRIORITY CONCERNING THE PURSUIT OF ACHIEVEMENTS?

Romans 12:3

As God's messenger, I give each of you this warning: Be honest in your estimate of yourselves, measuring your value by how much faith God has given you.

Mark 10:31

Many who seem to be important now will be the least important then, and those who are considered least here will be the greatest then.

Living by God's plan should be a higher priority than personal achievement.

WHAT ARE SOME TESTS TO DETERMINE MY PRIORITIES?

Proverbs 3:5-6

Trust in the LORD with all your heart; do not depend on your own understanding. Seek his will in all you do, and he will direct your paths.

Haggai 1:9

> You hoped for rich harvests, but they were poor. And when you brought your harvest home, I blew it away. Why? Because my house lies in ruins, says the LORD Almighty, while you are all busy building your own fine houses.

Luke 12:34

> Wherever your treasure is, there your heart and thoughts will also be.

Priorities are the scales on which our love for God is weighed. We focus most on what or whom we love most.

PROMISE FROM GOD:

Proverbs 3:6

> Seek his will in all you do, and he will direct your paths.

Procrastination

WHY DO I PROCRASTINATE?

Proverbs 6:10-11

> A little extra sleep, a little more slumber, a little folding of the hands to rest—and poverty will pounce on you like a bandit.

Procrastination is often a form of laziness and leads to disaster.

Joshua 18:3

> *How long are you going to wait before taking possession of the remaining land?*

Procrastination is sometimes a form of disobedience.

Matthew 25:25

> *I was afraid I would lose your money, so I hid it in the earth.*

We can be paralyzed by fear of failure and waste our resources through procrastination.

Ephesians 5:16

> *Make the most of every opportunity for doing good in these evil days.*

Time is a gift from God and must not be squandered.

Matthew 25:13

> *Stay awake and be prepared, because you do not know the day or hour of my return.*

Failure to be prepared for the coming of Christ is the most costly form of spiritual procrastination.

PROMISE FROM GOD:

Matthew 25:29

> *To those who use well what they are given, even more will be given, and they will have an abundance. But from those who are unfaithful, even what little they have will be taken away.*

Profanity

THEY'RE JUST WORDS. WHY IS PROFANITY SUCH A BIG DEAL?

Philippians 4:8

Fix your thoughts on what is true and honorable and right.
Think about things that are pure and lovely.

Our mind is to be filled not with the profane but with the holy.

Exodus 20:7

Do not misuse the name of the LORD your God.

To use the name of God frivolously is to violate God's standard
for holiness.

Exodus 21:17

Anyone who curses father or mother must be put to death.

To curse one's parents is as serious an offense as doing them
physical harm.

Ephesians 5:4

Obscene stories, foolish talk, and coarse jokes—these are not for
you. Instead, let there be thankfulness to God.

Foul language has no part in a believer's vocabulary.

PROMISE FROM GOD:

James 3:2

> Those who control their tongues can also control themselves in every other way.

Quitting

HOW CAN I KEEP GOING WHEN I FEEL LIKE QUITTING?

Nehemiah 4:2-3

> What does this bunch of poor, feeble Jews think they are doing? . . . That stone wall would collapse if even a fox walked along the top of it!

Faced with an overwhelming task and discouragement from adversaries, Nehemiah kept his eyes on the goal and his call.

Acts 20:22

> Now I am going to Jerusalem, drawn there irresistibly by the Holy Spirit, not knowing what awaits me.

Paul faced unimaginable hardship, yet he finished his course.

2 Corinthians 4:8

> We are pressed on every side by troubles, but we are not crushed and broken. We are perplexed, but we don't give up and quit.

Even in the midst of suffering, believers can find strength to endure for Christ.

2 Timothy 4:7

I have fought a good fight, I have finished the race, and I have remained faithful.

Matthew 10:22

Those who endure to the end will be saved.

Galatians 6:9

Don't get tired of doing what is good. Don't get discouraged and give up, for we will reap a harvest of blessing at the appropriate time.

We avoid discouragement by keeping our eyes on the goal and reward of heaven.

PROMISE FROM GOD:

Matthew 10:22

Everyone will hate you because of your allegiance to me. But those who endure to the end will be saved.

Racism

WHAT DOES THE BIBLE SAY ABOUT RACISM?

John 4:9

She said to Jesus, "You are a Jew, and I am a Samaritan woman. Why are you asking me for a drink?"

Although Samaritans were seen as half-breeds and were hated by the Jews of his day, Jesus went out of his way to have a life-changing conversation with one sinful Samaritan woman.

Luke 10:33
> *Then a despised Samaritan came along.*

Jesus confounded his listeners by making a despised Samaritan the hero of one of his most famous parables.

Colossians 3:11
> *In this new life, it doesn't matter if you are a Jew or a Gentile.*

The church of Jesus Christ should be color-blind.

Ephesians 2:14
> *Christ himself has made peace between us Jews and you Gentiles by making us all one people. He has broken down the wall of hostility that used to separate us.*

Christ died to destroy all the barriers of hostility that sin had created between people. We must not rebuild those walls.

PROMISE FROM GOD:
Galatians 3:28
> *There is no longer Jew or Gentile . . . for you are all Christians—you are one in Christ Jesus.*

Rape

WHERE WAS GOD, MY TOWER OF STRENGTH, MY REFUGE? DOESN'T HE CARE?

Psalm 55:17

> *Morning, noon, and night I plead aloud in my distress, and the LORD hears my voice.*

Psalm 118:5

> *In my distress I prayed to the LORD, and the LORD answered me and rescued me.*

Psalm 10:17

> *LORD, you know the hopes of the helpless. Surely you will listen to their cries and comfort them.*

Psalm 119:76

> *Now let your unfailing love comfort me, just as you promised me, your servant.*

We don't know why God allows tragedies to enter our life, but we do know that God hurts deeply with us and loves us more than we'll ever know. He comforts us and gives us the strength to work through our pain.

WHAT IS THE LORD'S RESPONSE TO RAPE?

Psalm 11:5

> The LORD examines both the righteous and the wicked. He
> hates everyone who loves violence.

Psalm 12:5

> The LORD replies, "I have seen violence done to the helpless,
> and I have heard the groans of the poor. Now I will rise up to
> rescue them, as they have longed for me to do."

God hates all violence, and he hates those who love violence.
They will surely be judged severely.

WHAT IS THE RELATIONSHIP BETWEEN EVIL DESIRES AND RAPE?

Romans 6:12

> Do not let sin control the way you live; do not give in to its
> lustful desires.

Galatians 5:19

> When you follow the desires of your sinful nature, your lives will
> produce these evil results: sexual immorality, impure thoughts,
> eagerness for lustful pleasure.

Ephesians 4:22

> Throw off your old evil nature and your former way of life,
> which is rotten through and through, full of lust and deception.

Lust and evil desires, left unchecked and uncontrolled, can lead to
immorality, violence, and rape.

DOES THE VICTIM OF A RAPE SHARE ANY RESPONSIBILITY FOR WHAT HAPPENED?

Deuteronomy 22:25-26

> If the man meets the engaged woman out in the country, and he rapes her, then only the man should die. Do nothing to the young woman; she has committed no crime worthy of death. This case is similar to that of someone who attacks and murders a neighbor.

Proverbs 16:29

> Violent people deceive their companions, leading them down a harmful path.

Proverbs 24:2

> They spend their days plotting violence, and their words are always stirring up trouble.

Rape is a violent act against an innocent victim. There is no excuse for such a terrible crime.

Deuteronomy 22:23-24

> If this happens within a town . . . the woman is guilty because she did not scream for help.

The victim of rape has a responsibility to try to protect herself in any way she can.

IS REVENGE THE ANSWER TO RAPE?

Genesis 34:2-25

> When the local prince, Shechem son of Hamor the Hivite, saw [Dinah], he took her and raped her. . . . Simeon and Levi took their swords, entered the town without opposition, and slaughtered every man there.

Simeon and Levi overreacted to their sister's rape and were harshly reprimanded by their father (Gen. 49:4-7).

Psalm 94:1

> *O LORD, the God to whom vengeance belongs, O God of vengeance, let your glorious justice be seen!*

Romans 12:19

> *Dear friends, never avenge yourselves. Leave that to God. For it is written, "I will take vengeance; I will repay those who deserve it," says the Lord.*

Leave revenge to God, for he is the Judge of the universe. A crime must be brought to justice, but personal revenge starts an endless cycle of sin and destruction.

HOW CAN I AVOID FEELINGS OF ANGER AND HATRED?

2 Samuel 13:11-29

> *As she was feeding him, he grabbed her and demanded, "Come to bed with me, my darling sister." "No, my brother!" she cried. "Don't be foolish! Don't do this to me! You know what a serious crime it is to do such a thing in Israel. . . ." But Amnon wouldn't listen to her, and since he was stronger than she was, he raped her. Then suddenly Amnon's love turned to hate. . . . When King David heard what had happened, he was very angry. And though Absalom never spoke to Amnon about it, he hated Amnon deeply because of what he had done to his sister. . . . So at Absalom's signal they murdered Amnon.*

Psalm 37:8

> *Stop your anger! Turn from your rage! Do not envy others—it only leads to harm.*

Ephesians 4:31-32

> Get rid of all bitterness, rage, anger, harsh words, and slander, as well as all types of malicious behavior. Instead, be kind to each other, tenderhearted, forgiving one another, just as God through Christ has forgiven you.

If we fill our heart and mind with God and his good things, we will empty our heart and mind of anger, hatred, and plotting violence.

HOW CAN THE ANSWER POSSIBLY BE FORGIVENESS—IS FORGIVENESS ABSOLUTELY NECESSARY?

Matthew 5:44

> Love your enemies! Pray for those who persecute you!

Mark 11:25

> When you are praying, first forgive anyone you are holding a grudge against, so that your Father in heaven will forgive your sins, too.

Matthew 18:21-22

> Peter came to him and asked, "Lord, how often should I forgive someone who sins against me? Seven times?" "No!" Jesus replied, "seventy times seven!"

Romans 12:21

> Don't let evil get the best of you, but conquer evil by doing good.

Christ forgave those who crucified him. There is nothing harder than forgiving someone who has greatly wronged you, but there is also nothing more healing.

PROMISE FROM GOD:

Revelation 21:4

> *He will remove all of their sorrows, and there will be no more death or sorrow or crying or pain. For the old world and its evils are gone forever.*

Rebellion

WHAT DOES IT MEAN TO REBEL AGAINST GOD?

Numbers 20:12

> *You did not trust me enough to demonstrate my holiness to the people of Israel.*

Moses rebelled when he did not trust God and disregarded God's instructions for Moses' leadership.

Jeremiah 1:16

> *They worship idols that they themselves have made!*

Matthew 6:21

> *Wherever your treasure is, there your heart and thoughts will also be.*

We rebel against God whenever we give our devotion to other things.

Judges 2.11-12
> *The Israelites . . . abandoned the LORD. . . . They chased after other gods, worshiping the gods of the people around them.*

When our rebellion leads to false worship, we are in peril of destruction.

Isaiah 59.2
> *Your sins have cut you off from God.*

1 John 3.4
> *Those who sin are opposed to the law of God.*

Sin is rebellion against God, wanting to do things our own way. When we rebel against God, we become separated from him.

1 Samuel 12.15
> *If you rebel against the LORD's commands and refuse to listen to him, then his hand will be as heavy upon you as it was upon your ancestors.*

Rebellion is refusing to listen to and obey God.

Ezekiel 20.13
> *They wouldn't obey my instructions even though obedience would have given them life.*

Sometimes our rebellion can be so stubborn that we refuse to obey even when obedience would spare our life.

Hebrews 3:12

> *Be careful then, dear brothers and sisters. Make sure that your own hearts are not evil and unbelieving, turning you away from the living God.*

The ultimate spiritual rebellion is refusing to accept the gracious offer of salvation through Jesus Christ.

Hosea 11:11

> *"I will bring them home again," says the LORD.*

No matter how far a rebel strays, God still loves that person with an everlasting love.

IS REBELLION EVER GOOD?

1 Peter 4:3

> *You have had enough in the past of the evil things that godless people enjoy.*

When under pressure to participate in sinful activities, the Christian must rebel against the crowd.

Matthew 21:12

> *Jesus entered the Temple and began to drive out the merchants.*

Jesus himself rebelled against systematic corruption in the temple.

PROMISE FROM GOD:

Jeremiah 3:22

> *"My wayward children," says the LORD, "come back to me, and I will heal your wayward hearts."*

Reconciliation

HOW CAN WE BE RECONCILED TO GOD?

Isaiah 53:5

He was wounded and crushed for our sins. He was beaten that we might have peace. He was whipped, and we were healed!

Romans 5:10

Since we were restored to friendship with God by the death of his Son while we were still his enemies, we will certainly be delivered from eternal punishment by his life.

Ephesians 2:13

Now you belong to Christ Jesus. Though you once were far away from God, now you have been brought near to him because of the blood of Christ.

Colossians 1:20-21

By him God reconciled everything to himself. He made peace with everything in heaven and on earth by means of his blood on the cross. This includes you who were once so far away from God.

Because Jesus Christ died for our sins, God has made it possible for us to be reconciled to him.

Romans 5:1

Since we have been made right in God's sight by faith, we have peace with God because of what Jesus Christ our Lord has done for us.

2 Corinthians 5:19-21

> *God was in Christ, reconciling the world to himself, no longer counting people's sins against them. This is the wonderful message he has given us to tell others. We are Christ's ambassadors, and God is using us to speak to you. We urge you, as though Christ himself were here pleading with you, "Be reconciled to God!" For God made Christ, who never sinned, to be the offering for our sin, so that we could be made right with God through Christ.*

Colossians 2:14

> *He canceled the record that contained the charges against us. He took it and destroyed it by nailing it to Christ's cross.*

In order to be reconciled with God, we must have faith in what Jesus Christ has done for us.

WHY IS RECONCILIATION BETWEEN PEOPLE IMPORTANT?

Matthew 5:23-24

> *If you are standing before the altar in the Temple, offering a sacrifice to God, and you suddenly remember that someone has something against you, leave your sacrifice there beside the altar. Go and be reconciled to that person. Then come and offer your sacrifice to God.*

Being reconciled to other people is important to our relationship with God.

Matthew 5:25-26

> *Come to terms quickly with your enemy before it is too late and you are dragged into court, handed over to an officer, and*

*thrown in jail. I assure you that you won't be free again until
you have paid the last penny.*

Working for reconciliation with others is wise.

Matthew 18:15

*If another believer sins against you, go privately and point out
the fault. If the other person listens and confesses it, you have
won that person back.*

God wants us to resolve our differences with others because
doing so promotes unity.

HOW CAN PEOPLE INVOLVED IN CONFLICT ACCOMPLISH RECONCILIATION?

Genesis 33:8-11

*"What were all the flocks and herds I met as I came?" Esau asked.
Jacob replied, "They are gifts, my lord, to ensure your goodwill."
"Brother, I have plenty," Esau answered. "Keep what you have."
"No, please accept them," Jacob said, "for what a relief it is to see
your friendly smile. It is like seeing the smile of God! Please take
my gifts, for God has been very generous to me. I have more than
enough." Jacob continued to insist, so Esau finally accepted them.*

Giving gifts can be an important part of being reconciled to
other people.

Ephesians 2:14

*Christ himself has made peace between us Jews and you Gentiles
by making us all one people. He has broken down the wall of
hostility that used to separate us.*

Through Christ, God has made a way for groups at enmity with one another to make peace and be fully reconciled.

Ephesians 1:10
> *This is his plan: At the right time he will bring everything together under the authority of Christ—everything in heaven and on earth.*

In Christ's kingdom there will be peace between all people.

PROMISE FROM GOD:
Colossians 1:21-22
> *You were his enemies, separated from him by your evil thoughts and actions, yet now he has brought you back as his friends. He has done this through his death on the cross in his own human body. As a result, he has brought you into the very presence of God, and you are holy and blameless as you stand before him without a single fault.*

Reliability: *see* **Responsibility**

Repentance

WHY DOES GOD WANT US TO REPENT?

Leviticus 26.40

> But at last my people will confess their sins and the sins of their ancestors for betraying me and being hostile toward me.

All of us need to repent because we have betrayed God with our sins.

2 Chronicles 30.9

> The LORD your God is gracious and merciful. If you return to him, he will not continue to turn his face from you.

Repentance is necessary for an ongoing relationship with God.

Proverbs 28.13

> People who cover over their sins will not prosper. But if they confess and forsake them, they will receive mercy.

Isaiah 55.7

> Let the people turn from their wicked deeds. Let them banish from their minds the very thought of doing wrong! Let them turn to the LORD that he may have mercy on them. Yes, turn to our God, for he will abundantly pardon.

Jeremiah 3:12

> *Therefore, go and say these words to Israel, "This is what the LORD says: O Israel, my faithless people, come home to me again, for I am merciful. I will not be angry with you forever."*

Repentance is necessary to receive God's mercy.

Ezekiel 18:30-32

> *I will judge each of you, O people of Israel, according to your actions, says the Sovereign LORD. Turn from your sins! Don't let them destroy you! Put all your rebellion behind you, and get for yourselves a new heart and a new spirit. For why should you die, O people of Israel? I don't want you to die, says the Sovereign LORD. Turn back and live!*

Ezekiel 33:11

> *As surely as I live, says the Sovereign LORD, I take no pleasure in the death of wicked people. I only want them to turn from their wicked ways so they can live. Turn! Turn from your wickedness, O people of Israel! Why should you die?*

Repentance is the key to having new life from God.

Matthew 3:2

> *Turn from your sins and turn to God, because the Kingdom of Heaven is near.*

Luke 24:47

> *There is forgiveness of sins for all who turn to me.*

Acts 2:37-38

> *Peter's words convicted them deeply, and they said to him and to the other apostles, "Brothers, what should we do?" Peter*

> replied, *"Each of you must turn from your sins and turn to God, and be baptized in the name of Jesus Christ for the forgiveness of your sins. Then you will receive the gift of the Holy Spirit."*

Forgiveness of sins and entrance to the kingdom of heaven is only for those who have turned away from their sins and turned to God.

Matthew 11:20-23

> *Jesus began to denounce the cities where he had done most of his miracles, because they hadn't turned from their sins and turned to God. . . . "You people of Capernaum, will you be exalted to heaven? No, you will be brought down to the place of the dead."*

Refusal to turn away from our sins will bring God's judgment.

PROMISE FROM GOD:

2 Chronicles 7:14

> *If my people who are called by my name will humble themselves and pray and seek my face and turn from their wicked ways, I will hear from heaven and will forgive their sins and heal their land.*

Reputation

SHOULD CHRISTIANS BE CONCERNED ABOUT THEIR REPUTATION?

2 Corinthians 8:20

> *We are anxious that no one should find fault with the way we are handling this generous gift.*

We must take care to build a reputation of integrity so that the testimony of Christ's Good News is not hindered.

Matthew 6:1

> *Don't do your good deeds publicly, to be admired.*

Jesus warns us not to pursue spirituality in order to impress others.

2 Peter 1:5

> *Your faith will produce a life of moral excellence.*

Any reputation we strive to achieve should result from being fully committed to building spiritual character in our life.

HOW CAN A BAD REPUTATION BE CHANGED?

1 Peter 2:12

> *They will see your honorable behavior, and they will believe and give honor to God.*

The surest way to influence the way others think of you is by your good behavior.

Deuteronomy 4:6

If you obey [God's laws] carefully, you will display your wisdom and intelligence to the surrounding nations.

Obedience to God brings a reputation for wisdom and intelligence.

Mark 2:16

They said to his disciples, "Why does he eat with such scum?"

Jesus doesn't accept us on the basis of our reputation. He accepts us because of his love, which can transform sinners.

3 John 1:3

Some of the brothers recently returned and made me very happy by telling me about your faithfulness and that you are living in the truth.

May we earn the reputation of living according to God's standards for purity and truth.

PROMISE FROM GOD:

1 Peter 5:6

Humble yourselves under the mighty power of God, and in his good time he will honor you.

Responsibility

How do I develop responsibility?

Matthew 25:20-26

> The servant to whom he had entrusted the five bags of gold said, "Sir, you gave me five bags of gold to invest, and I have doubled the amount." The master was full of praise. "Well done, my good and faithful servant. You have been faithful in handling this small amount, so now I will give you many more responsibilities. Let's celebrate together!" . . . Then the servant with the one bag of gold came and said, "Sir, I know you are a hard man, harvesting crops you didn't plant and gathering crops you didn't cultivate. I was afraid I would lose your money, so I hid it in the earth and here it is." But the master replied, "You wicked and lazy servant! You think I'm a hard man, do you, harvesting crops I didn't plant and gathering crops I didn't cultivate?"

Galatians 6:5

> We are each responsible for our own conduct.

We develop responsibility by conscientiously obeying God's word and doing what is right.

Romans 12:3

> As God's messenger, I give each of you this warning: Be honest in your estimate of yourselves, measuring your value by how much faith God has given you.

You can become more responsible by assessing how much responsibility you can handle and then making sure that you handle it well.

Proverbs 3:11-12

> *My child, don't ignore it when the LORD disciplines you, and don't be discouraged when he corrects you. For the LORD corrects those he loves, just as a father corrects a child in whom he delights.*

Hebrews 12:11

> *No discipline is enjoyable while it is happening—it is painful! But afterward there will be a quiet harvest of right living for those who are trained in this way.*

God will train you to be more responsible if you submit to his discipline and his work in your heart and life.

SHOULD I BE HELD RESPONSIBLE FOR THINGS THAT ARE NOT MY FAULT?

Genesis 3:12-13

> *"Yes," Adam admitted, "but it was the woman you gave me who brought me the fruit, and I ate it." Then the LORD God asked the woman, "How could you do such a thing?" "The serpent tricked me," she replied. "That's why I ate it."*

Genesis 16:5

> *Sarai said to Abram, "It's all your fault! Now this servant of mine is pregnant, and she despises me, though I myself gave her the privilege of sleeping with you. The LORD will make you pay for doing this to me!"*

Exodus 32:22-24

> *"Don't get upset, sir," Aaron replied. "You yourself know these*
> *people and what a wicked bunch they are. They said to me,*
> *'Make us some gods to lead us, for something has happened to*
> *this man Moses, who led us out of Egypt.' So I told them,*
> *'Bring me your gold earrings.' When they brought them to me,*
> *I threw them into the fire—and out came this calf!"*

Matthew 27:24

> *Pilate saw that he wasn't getting anywhere and that a riot was*
> *developing. So he sent for a bowl of water and washed his hands*
> *before the crowd, saying, "I am innocent of the blood of this*
> *man. The responsibility is yours!"*

Sometimes we try to pass the buck for things that we really *are*
responsible for.

1 Chronicles 21:7-8, 17

> *God was very displeased with the census, and he punished Israel*
> *for it. Then David said to God, "I have sinned greatly and*
> *shouldn't have taken the census. Please forgive me for doing this*
> *foolish thing." . . . And David said to God, "I am the one who*
> *called for the census! I am the one who has sinned and done*
> *wrong! But these people are innocent—what have they done?*
> *O LORD my God, let your anger fall against me and my family,*
> *but do not destroy your people."*

Sometimes it does seem that God is punishing the innocent for
the sins of the guilty. We should realize instead that innocent
people sometimes suffer the fallout of others' sins.

Numbers 14.20-23

The LORD said, ". . . As surely as I live, and as surely as the earth is filled with the LORD's glory, not one of these people will ever enter that land. They have seen my glorious presence and the miraculous signs I performed both in Egypt and in the wilderness, but again and again they tested me by refusing to listen. They will never even see the land I swore to give their ancestors. None of those who have treated me with contempt will enter it."

Deuteronomy 21.1-9

Suppose someone is found murdered in a field in the land the LORD your God is giving you, and you don't know who committed the murder. In such cases, your leaders and judges must determine which town is nearest the body. Then the leaders of that town must select a young cow that has never been trained or yoked to a plow. They must lead it to a valley that is neither plowed nor planted with a stream running through it. There they must break the cow's neck. The Levitical priests must go there also, for the LORD your God has chosen them to minister before him and to pronounce blessings in the LORD's name. And they are to decide all lawsuits and punishments. The leaders of the town nearest the body must wash their hands over the young cow whose neck was broken. Then they must say, "Our hands did not shed this blood, nor did we see it happen. O LORD, forgive your people Israel whom you have redeemed. Do not charge your people Israel with the guilt of murdering an innocent person." Then they will be absolved of the guilt of this person's blood. By following these instructions and doing what is right in the LORD's sight, you will cleanse the guilt of murder from your community.

Sometimes the whole community shares responsibility for the sins of one of its members.

Numbers 14:24

> *My servant Caleb is different from the others. He has remained loyal to me, and I will bring him into the land he explored. His descendants will receive their full share of that land.*

Those who are clearly innocent should not be punished with the guilty.

Deuteronomy 24:16

> *Parents must not be put to death for the sins of their children, nor the children for the sins of their parents. Those worthy of death must be executed for their own crimes.*

Ezekiel 18:1-4

> *Another message came to me from the LORD: "Why do you quote this proverb in the land of Israel: 'The parents have eaten sour grapes, but their children's mouths pucker at the taste'? As surely as I live, says the Sovereign LORD, you will not say this proverb anymore in Israel. For all people are mine to judge—both parents and children alike. And this is my rule: The person who sins will be the one who dies."*

In terms of judgment before God, a person is held responsible only for his or her own sins. God will not judge or punish you for someone else's sins. But unfortunately, sin's consequences affect others. Sin almost always hurts others and not just the sinner.

PROMISE FROM GOD:
Matthew 25:29

> *To those who use well what they are given, even more will be given, and they will have an abundance. But from those who are unfaithful, even what little they have will be taken away.*

Restlessness

I FEEL RESTLESS ABOUT MY FUTURE—WHOM I WILL MARRY AND WHAT JOB I WILL HAVE. IS IT WRONG TO WONDER ABOUT THESE THINGS?
Numbers 20:11

> *Moses raised his hand and struck the rock twice with the staff.*

Restlessness rooted in selfish impatience can lead us into sin.

1 Samuel 13:12

> *I felt obliged to offer the burnt offering myself before you came.*

When we disregard God's timing in favor of our own, we sometimes cut corners and displease God.

Ecclesiastes 1:13

> *I devoted myself to search for understanding and to explore by wisdom.*

A restless search for truth can lead to a deeper understanding of God and his purposes.

HOW DO I FIND PEACE?

Matthew 11:28
> *Jesus said, "Come to me, all of you who are weary and carry heavy burdens, and I will give you rest."*

Jesus promises his peace to all who come to him in trusting faith.

Romans 5:1
> *We have peace with God because of what Jesus Christ our Lord has done for us.*

Peace with God gives us peace of mind and heart.

Philippians 4:6-7
> *Pray about everything. . . . If you do this, you will experience God's peace.*

When we experience anxiety or restlessness, telling God our troubles will help us rest in faith and experience his peace.

PROMISE FROM GOD:

Philippians 4:6-7
> *Pray about everything. . . . If you do this, you will experience God's peace.*

Resurrection

HOW CAN I HAVE CONFIDENCE THAT GOD WILL SOMEDAY RESURRECT ME TO HEAVEN?

1 Corinthians 15:12-14

> *Tell me this—since we preach that Christ rose from the dead, why are some of you saying there will be no resurrection of the dead? For if there is no resurrection of the dead, then Christ has not been raised either. And if Christ was not raised, then all our preaching is useless, and your trust in God is useless.*

If Christ had not defeated death, there would be no hope for you or me. The fact that Christ *did* come back to life lends credence to God's promise to raise us from the dead.

WHAT DOES JESUS' RESURRECTION MEAN TO ME?

John 3:16

> *God so loved the world that he gave his only Son, so that everyone who believes in him will not perish but have eternal life.*

1 Corinthians 15:42

> *It is the same way for the resurrection of the dead. Our earthly bodies, which die and decay, will be different when they are resurrected, for they will never die.*

Jesus' resurrection was the essential aspect of God's plan to allow us to spend eternity with him. Because Jesus was raised from the dead, we can be assured that he has power over death and that we, too, will be resurrected one day and will live forever with him in heaven.

WHAT WILL OUR BODY BE LIKE AFTER IT IS RESURRECTED?

1 Corinthians 15:43-44

> *Our bodies now disappoint us, but when they are raised, they will be full of glory. They are weak now, but when they are raised, they will be full of power. They are natural human bodies now, but when they are raised, they will be spiritual bodies. For just as there are natural bodies, so also there are spiritual bodies.*

If you are disappointed with your body now, you won't be when you arrive in heaven. Our resurrected body will be full of power, strength, and vitality.

PROMISE FROM GOD:

John 11:25-26

> *Jesus told her, "I am the resurrection and the life. Those who believe in me, even though they die like everyone else, will live again. They are given eternal life for believing in me and will never perish."*

How does God want me to deal with ridicule?

2 Chronicles 30:10

> The messengers went from town to town throughout Ephraim and Manasseh and as far as the territory of Zebulun. But most of the people just laughed at the messengers and made fun of them.

Ridicule is nothing more than hurtful words designed to hurt another person.

Nehemiah 4:4

> I prayed, "Hear us, O our God, for we are being mocked. May their scoffing fall back on their own heads."

Nehemiah handled ridicule with prayer.

Matthew 5:11-12

> God blesses you when you are mocked and persecuted and lied about because you are my followers. Be happy about it! Be very glad! For a great reward awaits you in heaven. And remember, the ancient prophets were persecuted, too.

Realize that those who are faithful to God even through persecution will receive a great reward in heaven.

PROMISE FROM GOD:
1 Peter 4:14

> *Be happy if you are insulted for being a Christian, for then the glorious Spirit of God will come upon you.*

Salvation

WHAT DOES IT MEAN TO BE SAVED?
Romans 4:8

> *What joy for those whose sin is no longer counted against them by the Lord.*

Romans 3:24

> *God in his gracious kindness declares us not guilty.*

Being saved means no longer having our sins count against us. It means being forgiven by the mercy of God.

Psalm 103:12

> *He has removed our rebellious acts as far away from us as the east is from the west.*

Being saved means that our sins have been completely removed.

Psalm 51:9-10

> *Remove the stain of my guilt. Create in me a clean heart, O God.*

Being saved means that the stain of guilt has been washed away.

1 Peter 2:10
> *Once you received none of God's mercy; now you have received his mercy.*

Romans 3:24
> *He has done this through Christ Jesus, who has freed us by taking away our sins.*

Being saved means that we are forgiven in Christ.

HOW CAN I BE SAVED?

Romans 10:13
> *Anyone who calls on the name of the Lord will be saved.*

God's Word promises salvation to anyone who calls on Jesus' name.

John 3:16
> *God so loved the world that he gave his only Son, so that everyone who believes in him will not perish but have eternal life.*

John 5:24
> *I assure you, those who listen to my message and believe in God who sent me have eternal life.*

Jesus himself promised that those who believe in him will be saved.

Is salvation available to anyone?

John 3:16

> God so loved the world that he gave his only Son, so that everyone who believes in him will not perish but have eternal life.

Anyone can receive salvation by believing in Jesus Christ and his message of the Good News.

Hebrews 9:27

> It is destined that each person dies only once and after that comes judgment.

Salvation is available to all, but a time will come when it will be too late to receive it.

How can I be sure of my salvation?

John 1:12

> To all who believed him and accepted him, he gave the right to become children of God.

Just as a child cannot be "un-born," God's children—those who have believed in Jesus Christ—cannot be "un-born-again."

Romans 8:14

> All who are led by the Spirit of God are children of God.

The Holy Spirit takes up residence in our heart and assures us that we are God's children.

Matthew 14.30-31

> *"Save me, Lord!" he shouted. Instantly Jesus reached out his hand and grabbed him.*

We cannot save ourselves from sin, guilt, judgment, and spiritual death. Only Jesus Christ can save us.

WHY IS SALVATION SO CENTRAL TO CHRISTIANITY?

Genesis 6.11-13

> *The earth had become corrupt in God's sight. . . . So God said to Noah, "I have decided to destroy all living creatures."*

Romans 6.23

> *The wages of sin is death.*

Salvation is necessary because sin against a holy God separates us from him, bringing judgment and spiritual death.

Exodus 12.23

> *When he sees the blood on the top and sides of the doorframe, the LORD will pass over your home. He will not permit the Destroyer to enter and strike down your firstborn.*

Salvation through Christ is dramatically foreshadowed in the Passover lamb.

Acts 4.12

> *There is salvation in no one else! There is no other name in all of heaven for people to call on to save them.*

Because we are sinful, we need to be rescued—"saved"—from destruction. Jesus Christ provides this salvation when we call on him to save us.

PROMISE FROM GOD:

Romans 10:9

> *If you confess with your mouth that Jesus is Lord and believe in your heart that God raised him from the dead, you will be saved.*

Self-Control

WHY CAN'T I SEEM TO CONTROL CERTAIN DESIRES?

Galatians 5:24

> *Those who belong to Christ Jesus have nailed the passions and desires of their sinful nature to his cross.*

One reason for a lack of self-control may be that you haven't yet become God's child through faith in Jesus Christ. If that is the case, it is important to put your faith in him right away.

Romans 12:1

> *And so, dear brothers and sisters, I plead with you to give your bodies to God. Let them be a living and holy sacrifice—the kind he will accept.*

The way to become pure is to give ourselves completely to God. If we try to hang on to just a little sin, it will eventually rule us.

WHAT ARE SOME STEPS TO EXERCISING SELF-CONTROL?

Psalm 119:9

> *How can a young person stay pure? By obeying your word and following its rules.*

2 Timothy 2:5

> *Follow the Lord's rules for doing his work, just as an athlete either follows the rules or is disqualified and wins no prize.*

Self-control involves first knowing God's guidelines for right living as found in the Bible. You need to know what you must control before you can keep it under control. Regular, consistent reading of God's Word keeps God's guidelines for right living clearly before us.

Psalm 141:3

> *Take control of what I say, O LORD, and keep my lips sealed.*

Proverbs 10:19

> *Don't talk too much. . . . Be sensible and turn off the flow!*

Proverbs 13:3

> *Those who control their tongue will have a long life; a quick retort can ruin everything.*

Matthew 12:36

> *I tell you this, that you must give an account on judgment day of every idle word you speak.*

Ephesians 4:29

> *Don't use foul or abusive language. Let everything you say be good and helpful, so that your words will be an encouragement to those who hear them.*

James 1:26

> *If you claim to be religious but don't control your tongue, you are just fooling yourself, and your religion is worthless.*

We exercise self-control by watching what we say. How often we wish we could call back words as soon as they have left our mouth!

Romans 13:14

> *Let the Lord Jesus Christ take control of you, and don't think of ways to indulge your evil desires.*

2 Peter 1:6

> *Knowing God leads to self-control. Self-control leads to patient endurance, and patient endurance leads to godliness.*

We must ask God to help us with self-control. The better we know God, the easier self-control becomes.

WHEN WE NEED HELP BEYOND OUR OWN SELF-CONTROL, WHAT SHOULD WE DO?

Psalm 56:3-4

> *When I am afraid, I put my trust in you. O God, I praise your word. I trust in God, so why should I be afraid? What can mere mortals do to me?*

Psalm 60:12

> *With God's help we will do mighty things, for he will trample down our foes.*

Psalm 61:2

> *From the ends of the earth, I will cry to you for help, for my heart is overwhelmed. Lead me to the towering rock of safety.*

Our extremity is God's opportunity. When we face a problem or temptation, we should run to God for help.

SOMETIMES I FEEL AS IF I'M THE ONLY ONE WHO FACES TEMPTATIONS.
1 Corinthians 10:13

> *Remember that the temptations that come into your life are no different from what others experience. . . . When you are tempted, [God] will show you a way out so that you will not give in to it.*

It helps to know that others face the same temptations we do. It also helps to know that God wants to help us! Ask him.

WHAT ARE THE REWARDS OF SELF-CONTROL?
James 1:12

> *God blesses the people who patiently endure testing. Afterward they will receive the crown of life that God has promised to those who love him.*

God will reward in heaven those who practice self-control on earth.

PROMISE FROM GOD:
2 Peter 1:6

> *Knowing God leads to self-control. Self-control leads to patient endurance, and patient endurance leads to godliness.*

Sex/Sexuality

WHAT DOES GOD THINK ABOUT SEX?

Genesis 1.27-28

God created people in his own image; God patterned them after himself; male and female he created them. God blessed them and told them, "Multiply and fill the earth and subdue it."

Genesis 2.24

This explains why a man leaves his father and mother and is joined to his wife and the two are united into one.

God created the idea of sex. He made men and women as sexual beings—to reproduce and replenish the next generation and to use sex as a means of expressing love and delighting in one another. The sexual relationship is a key part of husbands' and wives' becoming one person. God intended sex to be a good thing within the context of a marriage relationship.

THE PREVAILING MODERN ATTITUDE ABOUT SEX BEFORE MARRIAGE SEEMS TO BE THAT AS LONG AS WE BOTH WANT TO DO IT, IT'S OK. WHAT DOES THE BIBLE HAVE TO SAY ABOUT PREMARITAL SEX?

1 Corinthians 7.2-3

Because there is so much sexual immorality, each man should have his own wife, and each woman should have her own husband. The husband should not deprive his wife of sexual intimacy, which is her right as a married woman, nor should the wife deprive her husband.

Hebrews 13:4

Give honor to marriage, and remain faithful to one another in marriage. God will surely judge people who are immoral and those who commit adultery.

Sexual intercourse is to be reserved for the commitment of marriage.

1 Thessalonians 4:3-4

God wants you to be holy, so you should keep clear of all sexual sin. Then each of you will control your body and live in holiness and honor.

The world's attitude says, "If it feels good, do it." God calls us to exercise control over our passions and our body. The fact that something feels good doesn't mean that we should do it. Instead, if it honors God, do it.

IS SEX IN MARRIAGE ONLY FOR REPRODUCTION, OR DID GOD PLAN FOR HUSBANDS AND WIVES TO ENJOY IT, TO DELIGHT IN ONE ANOTHER THROUGH SEX?

Proverbs 5:18-19

Rejoice in the wife of your youth. . . . Let her breasts satisfy you always. May you always be captivated by her love.

Song of Songs 7:6

Oh, how delightful you are, my beloved; how pleasant for utter delight!

Ephesians 5:28, 33

> *Husbands ought to love their wives as they love their own bodies. . . . So again I say, each man must love his wife as he loves himself.*

Sex is not only for reproduction but also for a bonding of love and for enjoyment between husbands and wives. It is an important way for a man and wife to experience intimacy.

Song of Songs 5:6

> *I opened to my lover, but he was gone. . . . I searched for him, but I couldn't find him anywhere.*

When marriage becomes routine, it is important to restoke the fires of sexual intimacy.

IS IT SO BAD IF I JUST THINK ABOUT SEX WITH SOMEONE? I DIDN'T REALLY DO IT.

Exodus 20:17

> *Do not covet your neighbor's house. Do not covet your neighbor's wife.*

Matthew 5:27-28

> *The law of Moses says, "Do not commit adultery." But I say, anyone who even looks at a woman with lust in his eye has already committed adultery with her in his heart.*

Lust is adultery in the heart. It is true that when you imagine having sex with someone, you have not consummated it with that person physically. But in your heart, you have.

WILL GOD FORGIVE MY PAST SEXUAL SINS? CAN I TRULY START OVER?

Acts 13:38-39

In . . . Jesus there is forgiveness for your sins. Everyone who believes in him is freed from all guilt and declared right with God.

God will forgive any sexual sin if there is true repentance, which involves turning away from that sin and seeking forgiveness.

Romans 1:24

God let them go ahead and do whatever shameful things their hearts desired.

God will not forgive sin when a person persists in that sin. Engaging in persistent, willful sin separates us from God.

BUT ISN'T MY BODY MY OWN, TO DO WITH AS I CHOOSE?

1 Corinthians 6:13

Our bodies were not made for sexual immorality. They were made for the Lord, and the Lord cares about our bodies.

1 Corinthians 6:19-20

Don't you know that your body is the temple of the Holy Spirit, who lives in you and was given to you by God? You do not belong to yourself, for God bought you with a high price. So you must honor God with your body.

When we become Christians, we dedicate ourselves to the Lord, and that includes our body. It is no longer truly ours, but rather it is his temple. In marriage our body belongs not to ourselves only but to our mate.

HOW CAN I FIGHT SEXUAL TEMPTATION? IT IS SO POWERFUL IN TODAY'S WORLD.

1 Corinthians 10:13

> *Remember that the temptations that come into your life are no different from what others experience. And God is faithful. He will keep the temptation from becoming so strong that you can't stand up against it.*

We can't fight sexual temptations by ourselves. They are too powerful. Cry out to God to help you. He can and he will.

Sin

WHAT ARE THE CONSEQUENCES OF SIN?

Exodus 34:7

> *I show this unfailing love to many thousands by forgiving every kind of sin and rebellion. Even so I do not leave sin unpunished.*

Leviticus 5:17

> *If any of them sin by doing something forbidden by the LORD, even if it is done unintentionally, they will be held responsible.*

Proverbs 11:21

> *You can be sure that evil people will be punished.*

Ecclesiastes 12:14

> *God will judge us for everything we do, including every secret thing, whether good or bad.*

Isaiah 13.11

> I, the LORD, will punish the world for its evil and the wicked for their sin.

Ezekiel 18.4

> The person who sins will be the one who dies.

Malachi 4.1

> The LORD Almighty says, "The day of judgment is coming, burning like a furnace. The arrogant and the wicked will be burned up like straw on that day. They will be consumed like a tree—roots and all."

Sin brings God's punishment because it is a violation of God's laws and his holiness.

Numbers 32.23

> You may be sure that your sin will find you out.

Proverbs 5.22

> An evil man is held captive by his own sins; they are ropes that catch and hold him.

Our sins come back on us. What you plant is what you harvest.

Isaiah 59.2

> There is a problem—your sins have cut you off from God. Because of your sin, he has turned away and will not listen anymore.

Sin has alienated us from God, so we are not able to enter his presence.

Luke 23:41
> *We deserve to die for our evil deeds.*

Romans 2:9
> *There will be trouble and calamity for everyone who keeps on sinning—for the Jew first and also for the Gentile.*

Romans 6:23
> *The wages of sin is death.*

Ephesians 2:1
> *Once you were dead, doomed forever because of your many sins.*

2 Thessalonians 1:9
> *They will be punished with everlasting destruction, forever separated from the Lord and from his glorious power.*

Revelation 20:15
> *Anyone whose name was not found recorded in the Book of Life was thrown into the lake of fire.*

The penalty for our sins is death—physical death and eternal judgment by God.

IS THERE A WAY TO BE FREE FROM SIN?

Psalm 19:12
> *How can I know all the sins lurking in my heart? Cleanse me from these hidden faults.*

Psalm 51:2-3
> *Wash me clean from my guilt. Purify me from my sin. For I recognize my shameful deeds—they haunt me day and night.*

Psalm 139:23-24

> *Search me, O God, and know my heart; test me and know my thoughts. Point out anything in me that offends you, and lead me along the path of everlasting life.*

Ask God to cleanse your heart from sin.

Isaiah 1:18

> *"Come now, let us argue this out," says the LORD. "No matter how deep the stain of your sins, I can remove it. I can make you as clean as freshly fallen snow. Even if you are stained as red as crimson, I can make you as white as wool."*

Zechariah 13:1

> *On that day a fountain will be opened for the dynasty of David and for the people of Jerusalem, a fountain to cleanse them from all their sins and defilement.*

Matthew 26:28

> *This is my blood, which seals the covenant between God and his people. It is poured out to forgive the sins of many.*

2 Corinthians 5:21

> *God made Christ, who never sinned, to be the offering for our sin, so that we could be made right with God through Christ.*

Hebrews 9:14

> *Just think how much more the blood of Christ will purify our hearts from deeds that lead to death so that we can worship the living God.*

God has made it possible for the stain of our sin to be removed through the shed blood of the Lord Jesus Christ.

Ezra 10:11

> *Confess your sin to the LORD, the God of your ancestors, and do what he demands.*

Isaiah 1:16

> *Wash yourselves and be clean! Let me no longer see your evil deeds. Give up your wicked ways.*

1 John 1:9

> *If we confess our sins to him, he is faithful and just to forgive us and to cleanse us from every wrong.*

Confessing our sins and turning away from them to obey God is the way to a right relationship with him. When we confess our sins to God, he forgives us and forgets our sins.

Romans 6:6, 18

> *Our old sinful selves were crucified with Christ so that sin might lose its power in our lives. We are no longer slaves to sin. . . . Now you are free from sin, your old master, and you have become slaves to your new master, righteousness.*

Galatians 5:24

> *Those who belong to Christ Jesus have nailed the passions and desires of their sinful nature to his cross and crucified them there.*

Because of what Christ has done, those who have faith in God are free from the power of sin.

PROMISE FROM GOD:

1 Peter 2:24

> He personally carried away our sins in his own body on the cross so we can be dead to sin and live for what is right. You have been healed by his wounds!

2 Peter 2:9

> The Lord knows how to rescue godly people from their trials, even while punishing the wicked right up until the day of judgment.

Singleness

CAN GOD HELP ME ACCEPT MY SINGLENESS?

1 Corinthians 7:7-8

> I wish everyone could get along without marrying, just as I do. But we are not all the same. God gives some the gift of marriage, and to others he gives the gift of singleness. Now I say to those who aren't married and to widows—it's better to stay unmarried, just as I am.

1 Corinthians 7:17

> You must accept whatever situation the Lord has put you in.

Sometimes when we desperately want something, we forget to see the gift of our current situation. Paul found that his singleness was an advantage in pursuing his call of establishing churches. Step back and look for ways God might use you in your current single state.

HOW CAN I DEAL WITH THE LONELINESS OF BEING SINGLE?

Matthew 28:20

> *I am with you always, even to the end of the age.*

We are never really alone. We can take comfort in the thought that God will never leave us.

1 Corinthians 7:32

> *In everything you do, I want you to be free from the concerns of this life. An unmarried man can spend his time doing the Lord's work and thinking how to please him.*

We can alleviate loneliness by focusing our attention on the things that God wants us to be doing and on the reality of Christ's presence with us.

HOW DO I AVOID BITTERNESS OVER BEING SINGLE?

Hebrews 12:15

> *Look after each other so that none of you will miss out on the special favor of God. Watch out that no bitter root of unbelief rises up among you, for whenever it springs up, many are corrupted by its poison.*

God tells us to look out for each other. Get involved with groups where you feel safe sharing your feelings and having people support you and pray for you.

PROMISES FROM GOD:

Psalm 68:6

> *God places the lonely in families.*

Ephesians 2:19

You are members of God's family.

Strengths and Weaknesses

HOW DO I KNOW WHAT MY STRENGTHS AND WEAKNESSES ARE?

Ephesians 1:16-17

I have never stopped thanking God for you. I pray for you constantly, asking God, the glorious Father of our Lord Jesus Christ, to give you spiritual wisdom and understanding, so that you might grow in your knowledge of God.

The more you know God, the better you will understand your own strengths and weaknesses.

Daniel 1:4

"Select only strong, healthy, and good-looking young men," he said. "Make sure they are well versed in every branch of learning, are gifted with knowledge and good sense, and have the poise needed to serve in the royal palace. Teach these young men the language and literature of the Babylonians."

Matthew 25:15

> *He gave five bags of gold to one, two bags of gold to another, and one bag of gold to the last—dividing it in proportion to their abilities—and then left on his trip.*

1 Timothy 4:14

> *Do not neglect the spiritual gift you received through the prophecies spoken to you when the elders of the church laid their hands on you.*

Our strengths will become evident to others around us and over us.

Exodus 31:3

> *I have filled him with the Spirit of God, giving him great wisdom, intelligence, and skill in all kinds of crafts.*

Romans 12:6

> *God has given each of us the ability to do certain things well. So if God has given you the ability to prophesy, speak out when you have faith that God is speaking through you.*

We should take a look at what God has gifted us to do.

PROMISES FROM GOD:

Isaiah 40:29-31

> *He gives power to those who are tired and worn out; he offers strength to the weak. Even youths will become exhausted, and young men will give up. But those who wait on the LORD will find new strength. They will fly high on wings like eagles. They will run and not grow weary. They will walk and not faint.*

Isaiah 41:10

> Don't be afraid, for I am with you. Do not be dismayed, for I am your God. I will strengthen you. I will help you. I will uphold you with my victorious right hand.

Success

How do I become truly successful?

Acts 16:31

> Believe on the Lord Jesus and you will be saved.

Having faith in Jesus is true success.

Matthew 22:37

> Jesus replied, "You must love the Lord your God with all your heart, all your soul, and all your mind."

True success involves wholehearted love for God.

1 Kings 2:3

> Observe the requirements of the LORD your God and follow all his ways.

Psalm 119:115

> I intend to obey the commands of my God.

Obedience to God's word brings true success.

Matthew 20:26

> *Among you it should be quite different. Whoever wants to be a leader among you must be your servant.*

Serving and helping others makes us successful in God's eyes.

Proverbs 16:3

> *Commit your work to the LORD, and then your plans will succeed.*

Committing all we do to God and putting him first in our life brings success.

Mark 4:19

> *All too quickly the message is crowded out by the cares of this life, the lure of wealth, and the desire for nice things.*

True success, which comes from God, is killed by our attraction to worldly things. When we lust for money, position, power, and fame, we will be tempted to spend our energies to get these things, and that will take us away from a pursuit of God.

IS IT OK TO TRY TO BE SUCCESSFUL IN THIS LIFE?

Proverbs 12:24

> *Work hard and become a leader; be lazy and become a slave.*

Proverbs 22:29

> *Do you see any truly competent workers? They will serve kings rather than ordinary people.*

There are many godly character traits that, if applied to life, often bring material success. These include hard work, integrity, commitment, serving others, and wisdom.

Genesis 39:2-3

> The LORD was with Joseph and blessed him greatly as he served in the home of his Egyptian master . . . giving him success in everything he did.

Exodus 33:14

> The LORD replied, "I will personally go with you . . . everything will be fine for you."

The Scriptures have frequent references to God's blessings for his people. God allows his people to have material blessing but urges them never to sacrifice spiritual riches for worldly wealth.

PROMISE FROM GOD:

Psalm 84:11

> The LORD God is our light and protector. He gives us grace and glory. No good thing will the LORD withhold from those who do what is right.

Suffering

WHY AM I SUFFERING? DOESN'T GOD CARE ABOUT ME?

Genesis 37:28

> When the traders came by, his brothers pulled Joseph out of the pit and sold him for twenty pieces of silver.

Jeremiah 32:18

> You are loving and kind to thousands, though children suffer for their parents' sins.

Sometimes we suffer because of the sins of others and not because of our own sins.

John 9.2-3

> *"Teacher," his disciples asked him, "why was this man born blind? Was it a result of his own sins or those of his parents?" "It was not because of his sins or his parents' sins," Jesus answered.*

Sometimes the suffering that comes to us is not our fault. The way we react to the suffering is the key.

Genesis 3.6, 23

> *The fruit looked so fresh and delicious. . . . So she ate some of the fruit. . . . The LORD God banished Adam and his wife from the Garden of Eden.*

Leviticus 26.43

> *At last the people will receive the due punishment for their sins, for they rejected my regulations and despised my laws.*

Proverbs 3.11-12

> *My child, don't ignore it when the LORD disciplines you. . . . For the LORD corrects those he loves, just as a father corrects a child in whom he delights.*

Sometimes God sends suffering as a consequence of our sins. He disciplines us because he loves us and wants to correct us and restore us to him.

Deuteronomy 8.2

> *Remember how the LORD your God led you through the wilderness for forty years, humbling you and testing you . . . to find out whether or not you would really obey his commands.*

Sometimes God tests us with suffering to encourage us to obey him.

1 Peter 4.14

> *Be happy if you are insulted for being a Christian, for then the glorious Spirit of God will come upon you.*

Sometimes we suffer because we must take a stand for Christ.

James 1.3

> *When your faith is tested, your endurance has a chance to grow.*

Sometimes we willingly suffer because it will help us grow and mature.

2 Timothy 3.12

> *Yes, and everyone who wants to live a godly life in Christ Jesus will suffer persecution.*

The world hates Christ, so when we identify with him, we can expect the world that inflicted suffering on him also to inflict suffering on us.

CAN ANY GOOD COME FROM SUFFERING?

Job 5.17-18

> *Consider the joy of those corrected by God! Do not despise the chastening of the Almighty when you sin. For though he wounds, he also bandages. He strikes, but his hands also heal.*

Suffering can bring great renewal and healing.

Romans 5:3-4

> *We can rejoice, too, when we run into problems and trials, for we know that they are good for us—they help us learn to endure. And endurance develops strength of character.*

2 Corinthians 1:5

> *You can be sure that the more we suffer for Christ, the more God will shower us with his comfort through Christ.*

2 Corinthians 12:10

> *Since I know it is all for Christ's good, I am quite content with my weaknesses and with insults, hardships, persecutions, and calamities. For when I am weak, then I am strong.*

2 Timothy 2:10

> *I am willing to endure anything if it will bring salvation and eternal glory in Christ Jesus to those God has chosen.*

Hebrews 12:11

> *No discipline is enjoyable while it is happening—it is painful! But afterward there will be a quiet harvest of right living for those who are trained in this way.*

James 1:3-4

> *When your faith is tested, your endurance has a chance to grow . . . for when your endurance is fully developed, you will be strong in character and ready for anything.*

When something is for our good, Christ's glory, and the building of his church, we should be happy to accept it even though it involves suffering.

HOW DO I STAY CLOSE TO GOD IN TIMES OF SUFFERING?

Psalm 22.24

> *He has not ignored the suffering of the needy. He has not turned
> and walked away. He has listened to their cries for help.*

Recognize that God has not abandoned us in times of suffering.

Psalm 126.5-6

> *Those who plant in tears will harvest with shouts of joy. They
> weep as they go to plant their seed, but they sing as they return
> with the harvest.*

Recognize that suffering is not forever. In the dark hours of the
night of suffering it is hard to think of a morning filled with joy
and gladness. But the tears of suffering are seeds that will sprout
in joy.

Lamentations 3.32-33

> *Though he brings grief, he also shows compassion according to
> the greatness of his unfailing love. For he does not enjoy hurting
> people or causing them sorrow.*

Recognize that God does not want to see us suffer. A loving God
does not enjoy the disciplines of life that must come our way.
But his compassionate love and care see us through our times of
discipline and suffering.

Matthew 17.12

> *Soon the Son of Man will also suffer at their hands.*

Luke 24:26

> *Wasn't it clearly predicted by the prophets that the Messiah would have to suffer all these things before entering his time of glory?*

John 3:16

> *God so loved the world that he gave his only Son, so that everyone who believes in him will not perish but have eternal life.*

Recognize that Jesus himself suffered for us. Christ suffered the agonies of the cross, which not only embraced incredible physical suffering but also the unthinkable suffering of bearing the sins of the world.

Romans 8:17-18

> *Since we are his children, we will share his treasures—for everything God gives to his Son, Christ, is ours, too. But if we are to share his glory, we must also share his suffering. Yet what we suffer now is nothing compared to the glory he will give us later.*

Hebrews 2:18

> *Since he himself has gone through suffering and temptation, he is able to help us when we are being tempted.*

When we share the suffering of Christ, we also share his treasures.

PROMISE FROM GOD:

2 Corinthians 1:3-4

> *All praise to the God and Father of our Lord Jesus Christ. He is the source of every mercy and the God who comforts us. He*

comforts us in all our troubles so that we can comfort others. When others are troubled, we will be able to give them the same comfort God has given us.

Suicide

WHAT DOES GOD SAY ABOUT SUICIDE?

Genesis 1:27

God created people in his own image; God patterned them after himself; male and female he created them.

1 Corinthians 6:20

God bought you with a high price. So you must honor God with your body.

Jesus paid the ultimate sacrifice for us so that we could have life. It would go against everything Jesus taught us to take our own life.

HOW CAN I DEAL WITH THOUGHTS OF SUICIDE?

Matthew 28:20

Be sure of this: I am with you always, even to the end of the age.

Remember that you are not alone.

Jeremiah 1.5

> *I knew you before I formed you in your mother's womb. Before you were born I set you apart and appointed you as my spokesman to the world.*

When you are tempted by thoughts of hopelessness, remember that God created you and has a plan for you.

Deuteronomy 4.29

> *You will search again for the LORD your God. And if you search for him with all your heart and soul, you will find him.*

Seek God, and you will find him and his purpose.

PROMISE FROM GOD:

Jeremiah 29.11

> *"I know the plans I have for you," says the LORD. "They are plans for good and not for disaster, to give you a future and a hope."*

Teamwork: *see* **Cooperation**

Temptation

Does temptation ever come from God?

James 1:13

> God is never tempted to do wrong, and he never tempts anyone
> else either.

Mark 7:21-22

> From within, out of a person's heart, come evil thoughts, sexual
> immorality, theft, murder, adultery, greed, wickedness, deceit,
> eagerness for lustful pleasure, envy, slander, pride, and
> foolishness. All these vile things come from within.

Temptation originates not from God but from within the heart
of a person.

James 1:2

> Whenever trouble comes your way, let it be an opportunity for
> joy.

Although God does not send temptation, he does delight in
helping us grow stronger through it.

What makes temptation so alluring?

Genesis 3:6

> The fruit looked so fresh and delicious. . . . So she ate some of
> the fruit.

Satan's favorite strategy is to make what is sinful appear to be desirable and good.

HOW CAN I AVOID FALLING INTO TEMPTATION?
Genesis 39:12

> *[Joseph] ran from the house.*

Often the best strategy against temptation is to flee the situation.

Proverbs 1:10

> *If sinners entice you, turn your back on them!*

Avoid following the advice or actions of sinful people.

Matthew 6:13

> *Don't let us yield to temptation.*

We should ask God to help us stand against temptation.

PROMISE FROM GOD:
1 Corinthians 10:13

> *Remember that the temptations that come into your life are no different from what others experience. And God is faithful. He will keep the temptation from becoming so strong that you can't stand up against it. When you are tempted, he will show you a way out so that you will not give in to it.*

Tolerance

WHAT THINGS SHOULD WE NEVER TOLERATE?

Deuteronomy 7:2-5

> *When the LORD your God hands these nations over to you and you conquer them, you must completely destroy them. Make no treaties with them and show them no mercy. . . . They will lead your young people away from me to worship other gods. Then the anger of the LORD will burn against you, and he will destroy you. Instead, you must break down their pagan altars and shatter their sacred pillars. Cut down their Asherah poles and burn their idols.*

We must never tolerate idolatry in our life. Our society has many idols—not statues but other gods—that people worship. We must never allow devotion to these idols to enter our heart or life.

2 Chronicles 18:1-2

> *Jehoshaphat enjoyed great riches and high esteem, and he arranged for his son to marry the daughter of King Ahab of Israel. A few years later, he went to Samaria to visit Ahab, who prepared a great banquet for him and his officials. They butchered great numbers of sheep and oxen for the feast. Then Ahab enticed Jehoshaphat to join forces with him to attack Ramoth-gilead.*

It was a grave mistake for Jehoshaphat to make a treaty with such a wicked man as King Ahab. So, too, we must never allow an attitude of tolerance to lead us into a position of moral or spiritual compromise.

Ezra 9:1

> *The Jewish leaders came to me and said, "Many of the people of Israel, and even some of the priests and Levites, have not kept themselves separate from the other peoples living in the land. They have taken up the detestable practices of the Canaanites, Hittites, Perizzites, Jebusites, Ammonites, Moabites, Egyptians, and Amorites."*

We should not tolerate pagan lifestyles among God's people.

Psalm 101:5

> *I will not tolerate people who slander their neighbors. I will not endure conceit and pride.*

We should not tolerate pride in ourselves.

Deuteronomy 12:30

> *Do not be trapped into following their example in worshiping their gods. Do not say, "How do these nations worship their gods? I want to follow their example."*

There is only one true God. We should not tolerate the worship of anything or anyone but God.

WHY IS TOLERANCE DANGEROUS?

1 Kings 11:3

> He had seven hundred wives and three hundred concubines.
> And sure enough, they led his heart away from the LORD.

Tolerance can lead us away from God.

PROMISE FROM GOD:

Deuteronomy 8:19

> I assure you of this: If you ever forget the LORD your God and
> follow other gods . . . you will certainly be destroyed.

Truth

WHO DETERMINES TRUTH?

2 Samuel 7:28

> You are God, O Sovereign LORD. Your words are truth.

Only God determines absolute truth.

MANY SAY THERE IS NO SUCH THING AS ABSOLUTE TRUTH. HOW DO WE KNOW THE BIBLE IS TRUE?

Psalm 119:160

> All your words are true; all your just laws will stand forever.

God's word is an extension of God's truthful character.

John 16:13
> *When the Spirit of truth comes, he will guide you into all truth.*

The Holy Spirit enlightens our mind and heart to the truth.

John 18:37
> *Jesus said . . . "I came to bring truth to the world. All who love the truth recognize that what I say is true."*

The human quest for truth finds its fulfillment in Jesus Christ.

1 John 1:1
> *We saw him with our own eyes and touched him with our own hands.*

We can trust the New Testament's claim of Christ's resurrection because the story is told by eyewitnesses.

DOES GOD REALLY EXPECT US TO TELL THE TRUTH ALL THE TIME?

Exodus 20:16
> *Do not testify falsely against your neighbor.*

God's law clearly forbids intentional lying.

Ephesians 4:15
> *We will hold to the truth in love.*

Followers of Christ are called to speak the truth always, in a loving manner.

PROMISE FROM GOD:

Psalm 119:160

> *All your words are true; all your just laws will stand forever.*

Values

HOW DO I CULTIVATE GODLY VALUES?

Genesis 39:8-9

> *Joseph refused. "Look," he told her, "my master trusts me with everything in his entire household. . . . How could I ever do such a wicked thing? It would be a great sin against God."*

Refuse to give in to what is wrong.

Matthew 7:12

> *Do for others what you would like them to do for you. This is a summary of all that is taught in the law.*

Galatians 5:22-23

> *When the Holy Spirit controls our lives, he will produce this kind of fruit in us: love, joy, peace, patience, kindness, goodness, faithfulness, gentleness, and self-control.*

Godly living is the fruit of God living in us.

Psalm 15:1-2

> *Who may worship in your sanctuary, LORD? . . . Those who lead blameless lives and do what is right, speaking the truth from sincere hearts.*

Micah 6:8

> *The LORD has already told you what is good, and this is what he requires: to do what is right, to love mercy, and to walk humbly with your God.*

Realize that God requires us to lead a godly life.

HOW DO I TAKE INVENTORY OF MY CURRENT VALUES?

Matthew 15:19

> *From the heart come evil thoughts, murder, adultery, all other sexual immorality, theft, lying, and slander.*

Romans 1:29

> *Their lives became full of every kind of wickedness, sin, greed, hate, envy, murder, fighting, deception, malicious behavior, and gossip.*

Ephesians 5:4

> *Obscene stories, foolish talk, and coarse jokes—these are not for you. Instead, let there be thankfulness to God.*

Proverbs 30:8

> *Help me never to tell a lie.*

Compare your current set of values with the values found in the Bible.

HOW IMPORTANT IS IT FOR US TO LIVE CONSISTENT MORAL LIVES?

Psalm 24:3-4

> *Who may climb the mountain of the LORD? Who may stand in his holy place? Only those whose hands and hearts are pure.*

Proverbs 28:2

> *When there is moral rot within a nation, its government topples easily.*

Strong moral values are essential to our own life with God and to the life of our society.

PROMISE FROM GOD:

Romans 5:3-5

> *We can rejoice, too, when we run into problems and trials, for we know that they are good for us—they help us learn to endure. And endurance develops strength of character in us, and character strengthens our confident expectation of salvation. And this expectation will not disappoint us. For we know how dearly God loves us, because he has given us the Holy Spirit to fill our hearts with his love.*

Virginity

What's so important about remaining a virgin until marriage?

Mark 10:6-9

> God's plan was seen from the beginning of creation, for "He made them male and female." "This explains why a man leaves his father and mother and is joined to his wife, and the two are united into one." Since they are no longer two but one, let no one separate them, for God has joined them together.

God made sex to form a permanent bond between a man and a woman in marriage. Virginity among those entering marriage helps ensure the integrity of this bond—that it will be strong and permanent.

2 Timothy 2:21

> If you keep yourself pure, you will be a utensil God can use for his purpose. Your life will be clean, and you will be ready for the Master to use you for every good work.

1 John 3:3

> All who believe this will keep themselves pure, just as Christ is pure.

We are called to purity in all areas of our life. Then God can use us most effectively to reach others.

CAN GOD FORGIVE ME FOR NOT STAYING A VIRGIN?

Acts 2.38

> Peter replied, "Each of you must turn from your sins and turn to God, and be baptized in the name of Jesus Christ for the forgiveness of your sins."

Acts 13.38

> In this man Jesus there is forgiveness for your sins.

God promises to forgive us when we sin. However, even after God has forgiven us, we still experience the consequences of our sin. In the case of premarital sex, the consequences can be long-term.

PROMISE FROM GOD:

Psalm 24.3-5

> Who may climb the mountain of the LORD? Who may stand in his holy place? Only those whose hands and hearts are pure. . . . They will receive the LORD's blessing and have right standing with God their savior.

Will of God: *see* God's Will

Wisdom

HOW DO WE OBTAIN WISDOM?

Job 28:28

> *The fear of the Lord is true wisdom; to forsake evil is real understanding.*

God gives wisdom to those who fear him and forsake evil.

1 John 2:27

> *You have received the Holy Spirit, and he lives within you, so you don't need anyone to teach you what is true. For the Spirit teaches you all things, and what he teaches is true—it is not a lie. So continue in what he has taught you, and continue to live in Christ.*

Wisdom comes from having a relationship with God.

Proverbs 1:5-6

> *Let those who are wise listen to these proverbs and become even wiser. And let those who understand receive guidance by exploring the depth of meaning in these proverbs, parables, wise sayings, and riddles.*

Obedience to God's Word—his commands, laws, and teachings—will make us wise.

Psalm 86:11

> *Teach me your ways, O LORD, that I may live according to your truth! Grant me purity of heart, that I may honor you.*

James 1:5

> *If you need wisdom—if you want to know what God wants you to do—ask him, and he will gladly tell you. He will not resent your asking.*

If you need wisdom, ask God, and he will give it.

Colossians 3:16

> *Let the words of Christ, in all their richness, live in your hearts and make you wise. Use his words to teach and counsel each other.*

Listening to Christ's teachings and obeying his words will give wisdom.

Proverbs 8:12, 17

> *I, Wisdom, live together with good judgment. I know where to discover knowledge and discernment. . . . I love all who love me. Those who search for me will surely find me.*

Those who seek wisdom are the ones who will find it.

PROMISE FROM GOD:

Proverbs 3:5-6

> *Trust in the LORD with all your heart; do not depend on your own understanding. Seek his will in all you do, and he will direct your paths.*

Witnessing

How do I overcome my fear of witnessing?

Exodus 4:12

> *Now go, and do as I have told you. I will help you speak well, and I will tell you what to say.*

Luke 21:15

> *I will give you the right words and such wisdom that none of your opponents will be able to reply!*

Trusting that God will speak through us will help us to overcome our fear of witnessing.

2 Corinthians 4:11, 13

> *Yes, we live under constant danger of death because we serve Jesus, so that the life of Jesus will be obvious in our dying bodies. . . . But we continue to preach because we have the same kind of faith the psalmist had when he said, "I believed in God, and so I speak."*

Even when we face death, faith in God can give us the courage to speak.

Psalm 27:1

> *The LORD is my light and my salvation—so why should I be afraid? The LORD protects me from danger—so why should I tremble?*

Isaiah 44:8

> *Do not tremble; do not be afraid. Have I not proclaimed from ages past what my purposes are for you? You are my witnesses—is there any other God? No! There is no other Rock—not one!*

Acts 18:9-10

> *One night the Lord spoke to Paul in a vision and told him, "Don't be afraid! Speak out! Don't be silent! For I am with you."*

Take courage and find strength in God's power, presence, and protection.

Ezekiel 2:6

> *Son of man, do not fear them. Don't be afraid even though their threats are sharp as thorns and barbed like briers, and they sting like scorpions. Do not be dismayed by their dark scowls. For remember, they are rebels!*

Be strong in God, and realize that rejection is just part of the territory.

John 12:26

> *All those who want to be my disciples must come and follow me, because my servants must be where I am. And if they follow me, the Father will honor them.*

Acts 4:18-20

> *So they called the apostles back in and told them never again to speak or teach about Jesus. But Peter and John replied, "Do you think God wants us to obey you rather than him? We cannot stop telling about the wonderful things we have seen and heard."*

Acts 5.40

> *The council accepted his advice. They called in the apostles and had them flogged. Then they ordered them never again to speak in the name of Jesus, and they let them go.*

Realize that when you witness you are following in Christ's and the apostles' footsteps.

Acts 1.8

> *When the Holy Spirit has come upon you, you will receive power and will tell people about me everywhere—in Jerusalem, throughout Judea, in Samaria, and to the ends of the earth.*

The Holy Spirit will empower us and help us to speak.

1 Corinthians 2.4

> *My message and my preaching were very plain. . . . But the Holy Spirit was powerful among you.*

1 Thessalonians 1.5

> *When we brought you the Good News . . . the Holy Spirit gave you full assurance that what we said was true.*

Go ahead and speak, and the Holy Spirit will work in people's heart and mind.

1 Thessalonians 2.4

> *Our purpose is to please God, not people. He is the one who examines the motives of our hearts.*

Focus on pleasing God rather than on pleasing people.

What do I do when people aren't interested in hearing about Christ?

Acts 17.32-34

> When they heard Paul speak of the resurrection of a person who had been dead, some laughed, but others said, "We want to hear more about this later." That ended Paul's discussion with them, but some joined him and became believers.

The majority may seem disinterested or hostile, but we don't know whether there are a few who will believe—so we should speak for their sake.

Ezekiel 2.5, 7-8

> Whether they listen or not—for remember, they are rebels—at least they will know they have had a prophet among them. . . . You must give them my messages whether they listen or not. But they won't listen, for they are completely rebellious! Son of man, listen to what I say to you. Do not join them in being a rebel. Open your mouth, and eat what I give you.

2 Timothy 4.2

> Preach the word of God. Be persistent, whether the time is favorable or not.

Even if attitudes or circumstances are not favorable, speak out anyway, and tell about Christ's work.

Luke 9.5

> If the people of the village won't receive your message when you enter it, shake off its dust from your feet as you leave. It is a sign that you have abandoned that village to its fate.

If, after we have told them the message, they refuse to accept it, leave them to their fate and keep going—there are many others to tell.

PROMISE FROM GOD:

Romans 10.15
> *How beautiful are the feet of those who bring good news!*

Words

WHAT KINDS OF WORDS SHOULD I SPEAK?

Genesis 50.21
> *He spoke very kindly to them, reassuring them.*

Speak kind words to others.

Psalm 50.23
> *Giving thanks is a sacrifice that truly honors me.*

Romans 15.6
> *All of you can join together with one voice, giving praise and glory to God, the Father of our Lord Jesus Christ.*

Speak words of thanks and praise to God.

Ephesians 4.29
> *Let everything you say be good and helpful, so that your words will be an encouragement to those who hear them.*

Use words that build others up.

Proverbs 15:4

> *Gentle words bring life and health.*

Proverbs 25:15

> *Patience can persuade a prince, and soft speech can crush strong opposition.*

Speak to others with gentleness.

1 Peter 3:9

> *Don't repay evil for evil. Don't retaliate when people say unkind things about you. Instead, pay them back with a blessing. That is what God wants you to do, and he will bless you for it.*

Use your words to bless even those who injure you.

Zechariah 8:16

> *This is what you must do: Tell the truth to each other. Render verdicts in your courts that are just and that lead to peace.*

Speak truthfully.

WHAT KINDS OF WORDS SHOULD I AVOID SPEAKING?

Exodus 22:28

> *Do not blaspheme God or curse anyone who rules over you.*

Never curse God or anyone in leadership over you.

Ecclesiastes 10:20

> *Never make light of the king, even in your thoughts. And don't make fun of a rich man, either. A little bird may tell them what you have said.*

Don't make fun of those in leadership.

Psalm 34:12-13

> *Do any of you want to live a life that is long and good? Then watch your tongue! Keep your lips from telling lies!*

Avoid saying anything that is deceptive or false.

Proverbs 18:8

> *What dainty morsels rumors are—but they sink deep into one's heart.*

Avoid spreading gossip or slander about other people.

Proverbs 29:11

> *A fool gives full vent to anger, but a wise person quietly holds it back.*

Avoid speaking in the heat of anger; you will usually regret it later.

James 4:11

> *Don't speak evil against each other, my dear brothers and sisters. If you criticize each other and condemn each other, then you are criticizing and condemning God's law.*

Avoid criticizing other people.

PROMISE FROM GOD:
Proverbs 10:11
> *The words of the godly lead to life.*

Work

WHAT KIND OF WORK SHOULD I DO?

Genesis 3:19
> *All your life you will sweat to produce food, until your dying day.*

Acts 20:34-35
> *You know that these hands of mine have worked to pay my own way, and I have even supplied the needs of those who were with me. And I have been a constant example of how you can help the poor by working hard.*

1 Corinthians 4:12
> *We have worked wearily with our own hands to earn our living.*

Ephesians 4:28
> *Begin using your hands for honest work, and then give generously to others in need.*

1 Timothy 5:8
> *Those who won't care for their own relatives, especially those living in the same household, have denied what we believe. Such people are worse than unbelievers.*

Plan on doing work that will enable you to provide for your own and your family's needs and to give generously to others.

Matthew 25:34-40

> *The King will say to those on the right, "Come, you who are blessed by my Father, inherit the Kingdom prepared for you from the foundation of the world. For I was hungry, and you fed me. I was thirsty, and you gave me a drink. I was a stranger, and you invited me into your home. I was naked, and you gave me clothing. I was sick, and you cared for me. I was in prison, and you visited me." Then these righteous ones will reply, "Lord, when did we ever see you hungry and feed you? Or thirsty and give you something to drink? Or a stranger and show you hospitality? Or naked and give you clothing? When did we ever see you sick or in prison, and visit you?" And the King will tell them, "I assure you, when you did it to one of the least of these my brothers and sisters, you were doing it to me!"*

Whatever you do, work for Christ's kingdom.

Matthew 5:16

> *Let your good deeds shine out for all to see, so that everyone will praise your heavenly Father.*

Do work that will cause other people to praise and glorify God.

Proverbs 13:11

> *Wealth from get-rich-quick schemes quickly disappears; wealth from hard work grows.*

Honest, hard work is much better than schemes to get rich quickly.

Romans 12:8

If your gift is to encourage others, do it! If you have money, share it generously. If God has given you leadership ability, take the responsibility seriously. And if you have a gift for showing kindness to others, do it gladly.

Do work that is in keeping with your gifts and abilities.

How should I work?

Proverbs 22:29

Do you see any truly competent workers? They will serve kings rather than ordinary people.

Ecclesiastes 9:10

Whatever you do, do well.

Be industrious, and do the best work you can.

Proverbs 10:5

A wise youth works hard all summer; a youth who sleeps away the hour of opportunity brings shame.

Work hard!

Ecclesiastes 10:10

Since a dull ax requires great strength, sharpen the blade. That's the value of wisdom; it helps you succeed.

Be smart in how you work.

Romans 12:11

Never be lazy in your work, but serve the Lord enthusiastically.

Ephesians 6:6-7

Work hard, but not just to please your masters when they are watching. As slaves of Christ, do the will of God with all your heart. Work with enthusiasm, as though you were working for the Lord rather than for people.

Work with enthusiasm at whatever you do, keeping in mind that you are serving God, not people.

James 3:13

If you are wise and understand God's ways, live a life of steady goodness so that only good deeds will pour forth. And if you don't brag about the good you do, then you will be truly wise!

Steadily do good work with an attitude of humility instead of continually pointing out your own accomplishments.

Titus 2:9-10

Slaves must obey their masters and do their best to please them. They must not talk back or steal, but they must show themselves to be entirely trustworthy and good. Then they will make the teaching about God our Savior attractive in every way.

Be trustworthy and faithful in your work.

Colossians 3:17

Whatever you do or say, let it be as a representative of the Lord Jesus, all the while giving thanks through him to God the Father.

Your goal should be to work in such a way that you are a good representative of Christ.

PROMISE FROM GOD:

Colossians 3:23-24

> Work hard and cheerfully at whatever you do, as though you were working for the Lord rather than for people. . . . The Lord will give you an inheritance as your reward.

Worry

WHEN DOES WORRY BECOME SIN?

Matthew 13:22

> The thorny ground represents those who hear and accept the Good News, but all too quickly the message is crowded out by the cares of this life.

Colossians 3:2

> Let heaven fill your thoughts. Do not think only about things down here on earth.

Worry is like thorny plants—both crowd out what is good. Our worry over the concerns of life becomes sin when it prevents the word of God from taking root in our life.

WHY DO I WORRY SO MUCH? HOW CAN I WORRY LESS?

Psalm 55:4

> My heart is in anguish.

Fear and anxiety are normal responses to threatening situations.

Exodus 14:13
> *Moses told the people, "Don't be afraid. Just stand where you are and watch the LORD rescue you."*

We combat worry and anxiety by remembering God's promises and trusting him.

Philippians 4:6
> *Don't worry about anything; instead, pray about everything.*

We combat worry by placing our cares in Jesus' hands.

Psalm 62:6
> *He alone is my rock and my salvation, my fortress where I will not be shaken.*

We find relief from fear in the promise of salvation.

Matthew 6:27
> *Can all your worries add a single moment to your life?*

Viewing our life from an eternal point of view helps us put our worries in the proper perspective.

PROMISE FROM GOD:
1 Peter 5:7
> *Give all your worries and cares to God, for he cares about what happens to you.*

Worship

Is worship important?

Exodus 34:8

> Moses immediately fell to the ground and worshiped.

2 Kings 17:36

> Worship only the LORD, who brought you out of Egypt with such mighty miracles and power. You must worship him and bow before him; offer sacrifices to him alone.

1 Chronicles 16:29

> Give to the LORD the glory he deserves! Bring your offering and come to worship him. Worship the LORD in all his holy splendor.

Psalm 145:3

> Great is the LORD! He is most worthy of praise! His greatness is beyond discovery!

Isaiah 66:1-2

> This is what the LORD says: "Heaven is my throne, and the earth is my footstool. Could you ever build me a temple as good as that? Could you build a dwelling place for me? My hands have made both heaven and earth, and they are mine. I, the LORD, have spoken! I will bless those who have humble and contrite hearts, who tremble at my word."

Worship is the recognition of who God is and of who we are in relation to him.

Genesis 35:1

> *God said to Jacob, "Now move on to Bethel and settle there. Build an altar there to worship me—the God who appeared to you."*

God has told his people to worship him.

Exodus 29:43

> *I will meet the people of Israel there, and the Tabernacle will be sanctified by my glorious presence.*

1 Kings 8:10-11

> *As the priests came out of the inner sanctuary, a cloud filled the Temple of the LORD. The priests could not continue their work because the glorious presence of the LORD filled the Temple.*

2 Chronicles 7:1

> *When Solomon finished praying, fire flashed down from heaven and burned up the burnt offerings and sacrifices, and the glorious presence of the LORD filled the Temple.*

God meets with his people in a powerful way when they worship him together.

Deuteronomy 31:11

> *You must read this law to all the people of Israel when they assemble before the LORD your God at the place he chooses.*

Micah 4:2

> *Come, let us go up to the mountain of the LORD, to the Temple of the God of Israel. There he will teach us his ways, so that we may obey him.*

Public corporate worship gives God's people an important opportunity to hear his Word proclaimed and to learn about God and his ways.

Psalm 5:7

> *Because of your unfailing love, I can enter your house; with deepest awe I will worship at your Temple.*

Psalm 47:7

> *God is the King over all the earth. Praise him with a psalm!*

Psalm 95:1

> *Come, let us sing to the LORD! Let us give a joyous shout to the rock of our salvation!*

Psalm 100:1-4

> *Shout with joy to the LORD, O earth! Worship the LORD with gladness. Come before him, singing with joy. Acknowledge that the LORD is God! He made us, and we are his. We are his people, the sheep of his pasture. Enter his gates with thanksgiving; go into his courts with praise. Give thanks to him and bless his name.*

Isaiah 6:3

> *In a great chorus they sang, "Holy, holy, holy is the LORD Almighty! The whole earth is filled with his glory!"*

Worship is a fitting response to God's holiness, power, and grace.

Matthew 14:33

> *Then the disciples worshiped him. "You really are the Son of God!" they exclaimed.*

Christ is worthy of our worship.

Revelation 4:9-11

> *Whenever the living beings give glory and honor and thanks to the one sitting on the throne, the one who lives forever and ever, the twenty-four elders fall down and worship the one who lives forever and ever. And they lay their crowns before the throne and say, "You are worthy, O Lord our God, to receive glory and honor and power. For you created everything, and it is for your pleasure that they exist and were created."*

Revelation 5:11-12

> *I looked again, and I heard the singing of thousands and millions of angels around the throne and the living beings and the elders. And they sang in a mighty chorus: "The Lamb is worthy—the Lamb who was killed. He is worthy to receive power and riches and wisdom and strength and honor and glory and blessing."*

Our worship of God is a foretaste of heaven.

How should I worship God?

Genesis 35:2-3

> *Jacob told everyone in his household, "Destroy your idols, wash yourselves, and put on clean clothing. We are now going to Bethel, where I will build an altar to the God who answered my prayers when I was in distress. He has stayed with me wherever I have gone."*

Exodus 20:2-4

> *I am the LORD your God, who rescued you from slavery in Egypt. Do not worship any other gods besides me. Do not make idols of any kind, whether in the shape of birds or animals or fish.*

Deuteronomy 11:16

> *Do not let your heart turn away from the LORD to worship other gods.*

Revelation 22:9

> *He said, "No, don't worship me. I am a servant of God, just like you and your brothers the prophets, as well as all who obey what is written in this scroll. Worship God!"*

We must worship only God!

Exodus 3:5

> *"Do not come any closer," God told him. "Take off your sandals, for you are standing on holy ground."*

When we enter God's presence in worship, we should recognize that we are standing on holy ground.

Psalm 9:11

> *Sing praises to the LORD who reigns in Jerusalem. Tell the world about his unforgettable deeds.*

Psalm 35:18

> *I will thank you in front of the entire congregation. I will praise you before all the people.*

Hebrews 13:15

> *With Jesus' help, let us continually offer our sacrifice of praise to God by proclaiming the glory of his name.*

Our worship should include giving praise and thanks to God for what he has done.

Psalm 30:4

> *Sing to the LORD, all you godly ones! Praise his holy name.*

Psalm 147:1

> *Praise the LORD! How good it is to sing praises to our God! How delightful and how right!*

Ephesians 5:19

> *You will sing psalms and hymns and spiritual songs among yourselves, making music to the Lord in your hearts.*

Singing is an important part of our worship to God.

Psalm 33:2

> *Praise the LORD with melodies on the lyre; make music for him on the ten-stringed harp.*

Psalm 71:22

> *I will praise you with music on the harp, because you are faithful to your promises, O God. I will sing for you with a lyre, O Holy One of Israel.*

Psalm 150:3-5

> *Praise him with a blast of the trumpet; praise him with the lyre and harp! Praise him with the tambourine and dancing; praise him with stringed instruments and flutes! Praise him with a clash of cymbals; praise him with loud clanging cymbals.*

Musical instruments play an important role in our worship.

Deuteronomy 31.12-13

Call them all together—men, women, children, and the foreigners living in your towns—so they may listen and learn to fear the LORD your God and carefully obey all the terms of this law. Do this so that your children who have not known these laws will hear them and will learn to fear the LORD your God. Do this as long as you live in the land you are crossing the Jordan to occupy.

2 Chronicles 20.13

All the men of Judah stood before the LORD with their little ones, wives, and children.

It is good for everyone in the family to be present together for worship.

1 Chronicles 13.8

David and all Israel were celebrating before God with all their might, singing and playing all kinds of musical instruments— lyres, harps, tambourines, cymbals, and trumpets.

Worship can take the form of a joyous celebration with instruments of music.

1 Chronicles 15.16

David also ordered the Levite leaders to appoint a choir of Levites who were singers and musicians to sing joyful songs to the accompaniment of lyres, harps, and cymbals.

A choir can aid in worship.

1 Chronicles 16:4

> *David appointed the following Levites to lead the people in worship before the Ark of the LORD by asking for his blessings and giving thanks and praise to the LORD, the God of Israel.*

Worship leaders can help guide God's people in worship.

Psalm 95:6

> *Come, let us worship and bow down. Let us kneel before the LORD our maker.*

Kneeling and bowing are appropriate postures for worship.

Hebrews 12:28

> *Since we are receiving a Kingdom that cannot be destroyed, let us be thankful and please God by worshiping him with holy fear and awe.*

Holy fear and awe should accompany thanksgiving as our attitude in worship.

1 Chronicles 29:10-13

> *David praised the LORD in the presence of the whole assembly: "O LORD, the God of our ancestor Israel, may you be praised forever and ever! Yours, O LORD, is the greatness, the power, the glory, the victory, and the majesty. Everything in the heavens and on earth is yours, O LORD, and this is your kingdom. We adore you as the one who is over all things. Riches and honor come from you alone, for you rule over everything. Power and might are in your hand, and it is at your discretion that people are made great and given strength. O our God, we thank you and praise your glorious name!"*

1 Timothy 2:8

> *Wherever you assemble, I want men to pray with holy hands lifted up to God, free from anger and controversy.*

Public prayer is an important part of corporate worship.

Amos 5:21-24

> *I hate all your show and pretense—the hypocrisy of your religious festivals and solemn assemblies. I will not accept your burnt offerings and grain offerings. I won't even notice all your choice peace offerings. Away with your hymns of praise! They are only noise to my ears. I will not listen to your music, no matter how lovely it is. Instead, I want to see a mighty flood of justice, a river of righteous living that will never run dry.*

Public worship conducted with hypocrisy and unrighteousness is worse than useless.

Matthew 2:11

> *They entered the house where the child and his mother, Mary, were, and they fell down before him and worshiped him. Then they opened their treasure chests and gave him gifts of gold, frankincense, and myrrh.*

Worship should be accompanied by giving.

Acts 2:46

> *They worshiped together at the Temple each day, met in homes for the Lord's Supper, and shared their meals with great joy and generosity.*

1 Corinthians 11:23-26

> *This is what the Lord himself said, and I pass it on to you just as I received it. On the night when he was betrayed, the Lord Jesus took a loaf of bread, and when he had given thanks, he broke it and said, "This is my body, which is given for you. Do this in remembrance of me." In the same way, he took the cup of wine after supper, saying, "This cup is the new covenant between God and you, sealed by the shedding of my blood. Do this in remembrance of me as often as you drink it." For every time you eat this bread and drink this cup, you are announcing the Lord's death until he comes again.*

The Lord's Supper is both an act of worship to God and an act of fellowship among believers.

PROMISES FROM GOD:

Psalm 66:4

> *Everything on earth will worship you; they will sing your praises, shouting your name in glorious songs.*

Revelation 15:4

> *Who will not fear, O Lord, and glorify your name? For you alone are holy. All nations will come and worship before you, for your righteous deeds have been revealed.*

OF WHAT IS GOD WORTHY?

2 Samuel 22.4

I will call on the LORD, who is worthy of praise, for he saves me from my enemies.

Psalm 29.1-2

Give honor to the LORD, you angels; give honor to the LORD for his glory and strength. Give honor to the LORD for the glory of his name. Worship the LORD in the splendor of his holiness.

Psalm 33.4

The word of the LORD holds true, and everything he does is worthy of our trust.

Psalm 145.3

Great is the LORD! He is most worthy of praise! His greatness is beyond discovery!

Revelation 4.11

You are worthy, O Lord our God, to receive glory and honor and power. For you created everything, and it is for your pleasure that they exist and were created.

God is worthy of our praise, worship, respect, and trust.

WHAT AM I WORTH—WHAT IS MY VALUE TO GOD?
Deuteronomy 26:18
> *The LORD has declared today that you are his people, his own special treasure, just as he promised, and that you must obey all his commands.*

Psalm 8:5
> *You made us only a little lower than God, and you crowned us with glory and honor.*

God declares us very valuable to him.

WHAT MAKES ME WORTHY?
Genesis 1:27
> *God created people in his own image; God patterned them after himself; male and female he created them.*

Each of us is created in God's image. This makes us very valuable.

WHAT DOES GOD CONSIDER TO BE WORTHWHILE OR VALUABLE?
1 Corinthians 13:13
> *There are three things that will endure—faith, hope, and love—and the greatest of these is love.*

Faith, hope, and love have enduring value.

Proverbs 4:7
> *Getting wisdom is the most important thing you can do! And whatever else you do, get good judgment.*

Wisdom and good judgment are extremely worthwhile.

Ecclesiastes 7:1
> *A good reputation is more valuable than the most expensive perfume.*

A good reputation has great value.

Proverbs 20:15
> *Wise speech is rarer and more valuable than gold and rubies.*

Wise and helpful words are very valuable.

HOW CAN I KEEP MY LIFE FOCUSED ON THINGS OF WORTH?

Psalm 119:37
> *Turn my eyes from worthless things, and give me life through your word.*

Acts 14:15
> *We have come to bring you the Good News that you should turn from these worthless things to the living God, who made heaven and earth, the sea, and everything in them.*

Acts 20:24
> *My life is worth nothing unless I use it for doing the work assigned me by the Lord Jesus—the work of telling others the Good News about God's wonderful kindness and love.*

2 Corinthians 3:5
> *It is not that we think we can do anything of lasting value by ourselves. Our only power and success come from God.*

Philippians 3:8

> Yes, everything else is worthless when compared with the priceless gain of knowing Christ Jesus my Lord. I have discarded everything else, counting it all as garbage, so that I may have Christ.

Philippians 4:8

> Dear brothers and sisters, let me say one more thing as I close this letter. Fix your thoughts on what is true and honorable and right. Think about things that are pure and lovely and admirable. Think about things that are excellent and worthy of praise.

When we focus on Christ, the Word of God, heaven, and doing God's work for his kingdom, we ensure that the focus of our life is worthwhile.

PROMISE FROM GOD:

Psalm 8:5

> You made us only a little lower than God, and you crowned us with glory and honor.

INDEX

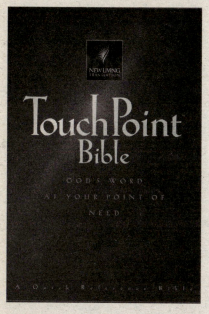

If you enjoyed TouchPoints for Graduates, you will love the TouchPoint Bible.

The *TouchPoint Bible* is the most helpful Bible available for finding just the right Bible verses to meet an immediate need in your life or in the life of someone you are trying to help. With the exclusive HelpFinder Index, you have instant access to hundreds of key topics and thousands of Bible verses. The *TouchPoint Bible* also includes book introductions and Bible promises as well as hundreds of in-text application notes to help you apply God's truth to everyday life. Make the *TouchPoint Bible* your favorite Bible for church, devotional reading, or study.